Income
Growth
With
Security

THE FORMULA-PLAN SOLUTION

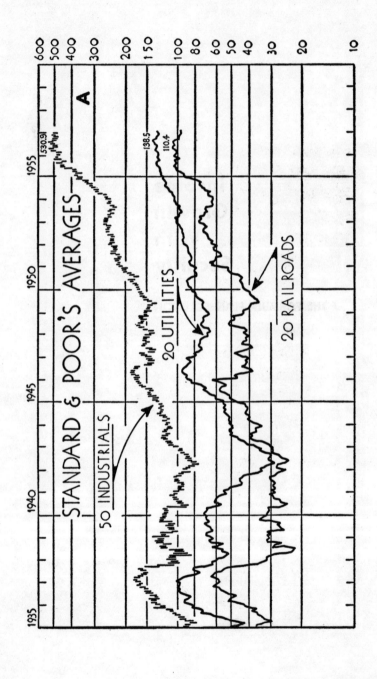

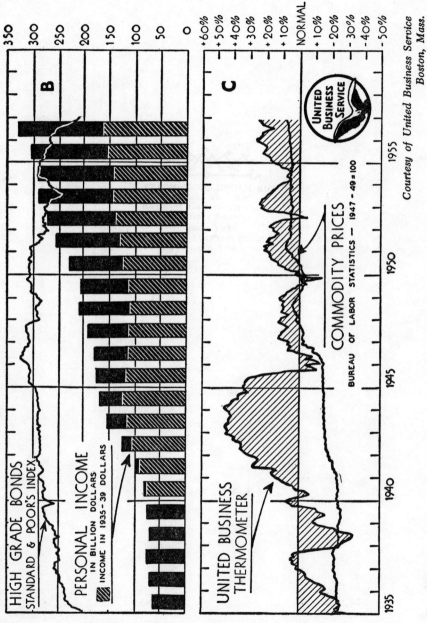

HIGH GRADE BONDS
STANDARD & POOR'S INDEX

B

PERSONAL INCOME
IN BILLION DOLLARS
▨ INCOME IN 1935-39 DOLLARS

350
300
250
200
150
100
50
0

+60%
+50%
+40%
+30%
+20%
+10%
NORMAL
- 10%
- 20%
- 30%
- 40%
- 50%

C

UNITED BUSINESS
THERMOMETER

COMMODITY PRICES
BUREAU OF LABOR STATISTICS — 1947-49=100

UNITED
BUSINESS
SERVICE

1935   1940   1945   1950   1955

Courtesy of United Business Service
Boston, Mass.

Frontispiece

THE MACMILLAN COMPANY
NEW YORK · CHICAGO
DALLAS · ATLANTA · SAN FRANCISCO
LONDON · MANILA

IN CANADA
BRETT-MACMILLAN LTD.
GALT, ONTARIO

Sherman F. Feyler

Income
Growth
With
Security

THE FORMULA-PLAN SOLUTION

THE MACMILLAN COMPANY · NEW YORK

To My Father

Whose own successful example in the business
and financial world and whose wise counsel
and encouragement over the years persuaded
me to seek a career in finance, a field which
for me has continually proved to be intensely
stimulating, mentally challenging, and gener-
ously rewarding.

Preface

The author, recognizing the many difficulties and hazards involved in any attempt to solve the problem of investment, provides in this book an analysis of a relatively new technique for investment that has already demonstrated its worth. This technique has come to be known as the formula-plan method. Since the fall of 1946, when it first came into prominence—at a time when many individual and institutional investors became disheartened by the downswing in stock prices after World War II and sought protection against the severe extremities of market fluctuations—the method has gained increasing favor.

Successful investment, broadly speaking, has two aspects: one of *selection* and the other of *timing*. Selection, which relates to the choice of securities to be bought or sold, generally involves the entire field of security analysis. Timing, which deals with the particular points in time at which to buy or sell the securities previously selected, covers broadly the whole body of research known as price analysis. The successful investor must have some degree of expertness in both selection and timing. Even though he may make a reasonably good selection of securities, he may suffer losses because of improper timing. Contrariwise, if he is sufficiently clairvoyant to time his buying and selling properly, he may yet incur losses because of improper selection. The successful investor will have not only the equipment with which to master both problems but will have also the skill required to operate the equipment for maximum results.

It is the author's personal observation that the problem of timing presents greater difficulty than that of selection; timing is likely not only to prove more mysterious but also to present more pitfalls to the unwary investor. Timing is a more perplexing problem largely because it essentially involves a forecast of the future—and few individuals are capable of accurately predicting cyclical security price movements.

Certainly it cannot be denied that an investor may be able to hit a top or a bottom in the price movement fairly well at one time and another, but to do so consistently is inconceivable. Since the experts are frequently wrong in their forecasts, how can investors aspire to even approximately correct timing! If stock market price movements were less sensitive than they actually are or if they followed in rhythmical sequence the fluctuations of some still more sensitive index, the process of forecasting would be less susceptible to error. But the fact is that stock prices generally foreshadow coming economic developments; consequently, they tend to move earlier and much faster than many other business indices.

In an attempt to help the investor improve the timing of his security purchases and sales, the author has dealt at length with the various factors that bear upon the problem. The opening chapter of the book states the problem, tells how it has been approached in the past, what can be expected from the usual methods of forecasting, and what factors related to proper timing have previously been thought important. Next, certain basic characteristics and the major implications of the formula-plan method are carefully considered, and the fundamental principles which govern the two major categories of formula plans—equalization plans and variable-ratio plans —are elaborated in detail.

Important institutional adaptations of the variable-ratio idea are discussed before problems of the individual investor in connection with its application are taken up in detail. Since no analysis of the formula-plan method would be complete without reference to the somewhat elementary, yet potentially productive process—dollar cost averaging—of building an investment fund over a period of time, the method of dollar averaging is treated fully. The description of major features in the so-called Monthly Investment Plan (M.I.P.), sponsored by the New York Stock Exchange, should be of substantial assistance to many readers. The critical evaluation of the formula-plan method, as well as its major difficulties and limitations—particularly as they concern the anticipation of the long-term trend of stock prices—should prove valuable to any person or group desiring to increase income while minimizing risk. In the final chapter, the main lines of argument are summarized, and the relative effectiveness of the formula-plan method is compared with other investment-timing methods applicable to varying types of security price fluctuation.

SHERMAN F. FEYLER

Assistant Professor of Finance
University of Buffalo

Contents

Figures

Figures

Tables

Chapter 1

The Search for Proper Timing

DIVERSIFICATION

The average investor who seeks guidance on his investment program will probably be told by his financial counselor to diversify. The principles of diversification have been advocated for years by those who consider themselves expert in the investment profession. Diversification was to be the starting point—the basic foundation— from which the investor should proceed in the commitment of his funds. The policy became firmly entrenched over the years, and its unquestioned acceptance became widespread in the field of investment counsel.

Everyone was, and still is, being told that to achieve safety of principal and of income, as well as to leave some hope and opportunity, perhaps, for capital appreciation, he should spread his risks, i.e., diversify. Diversification was recommended along four major lines:

1. The investor should spread his commitments over several different industries.

2. He should purchase the securities of several different companies within those industries.

3. He should spread his commitments, in some agreeable proportions, over several different kinds of securities available, such as bonds (both governmental and corporate), preferred stocks, and common stocks.

4. He should not concentrate his holdings too heavily in one geographical area but rather should spread them over several different geographical areas.

Diversification *per se* is sound both in theory and in fact. Spreading the risks of investment in the four ways listed above helps to safeguard not only the safety of the principal but also the continuity of the income derived from the investments. Requiring that some part of the investment fund be committed to common stocks helps to protect the investor against the injury that a period of commodity-price inflation could inflict upon the purchasing power of a fund committed wholly to fixed-income securities. Moreover, such a requirement tends to balance losses against gains and thus helps to preserve the integrity of the original corpus of the fund. In the field of investment, some losses are perhaps inevitable and unavoidable, as are also some gains. No one can know with certitude what lies in the future. Diversification recognizes that losses are unavoidable and attempts to minimize them, despite the source from which they may arrive—industry or company, price-level change, geographical concentration, or time of purchase.

However, diversification while reducing risk does not eliminate it. In achieving what he thinks is adequate diversification, the investor should not allow himself to be lulled into a false sense of security. He must not blind himself to the fact that he is still assuming risk, if only because the future is unpredictable. The experience of the past may point toward or suggest a future course of events, but it cannot definitely predict it.

Finally, diversification is a relative matter. What do we mean by proper or adequate diversification? A great deal has to do with the size of the investment fund available, as well as with the desires, needs, and preferences of the individual. Diversification should not be carried to such a foolhardy extreme that it involves the investor in an impossible amount of supervision. It is difficult to prescribe exact rules but, as an example, a fund of $100,000 might properly be spread over 20 or 25 different issues. A small fund, say under $10,000, might achieve adequate diversification by restriction to the purchase of investment-trust shares or shares in open-end mutual funds. However, it should be pointed out in this connection that more good selection and less diversification might achieve greater potential capital gain. Recently there seems to be a growing body of opinion in favor of limiting diversification to relatively few issues but making sure that those few not only are the best available at the moment but are given the most careful and continuous scrutiny thereafter.

If the investor refused to accept the guidance offered by the precepts of diversification, he would deliberately invite dangers and risks that a conservative person should not assume. In the attempt to maximize his gain, he would concentrate his risks too heavily in one or a few situations, and he would expose himself to serious loss of principal if a sudden adverse economic development threatened the safety of the one or the few situations to which he was committed. In order to be successful, he would, if he did not diversify, also necessarily face the difficulty of having to make correct forecasts of the price prospects of the issue to which he committed his funds. For, if it were possible for anyone to *consistently* make correct forecasts, he would not have to bother with diversification; he would be in the enviable position of always being able to maximize his gain. He would always purchase the *one* company's securities, in the *one* industry, in the *one* geographical area that would, on the basis of his forecast, produce the greatest gain. He would also need to hold at any one time only one type of security, for our hypothetical forecaster would always be able to predict tops and bottoms in the market—the end of bull markets as well as of bear markets—and for maximum gain he would buy all common stocks at the end of a bear market and switch into bonds or some other type of security less susceptible to price fluctuation at the top of a bull market.

LIMITATIONS OF MARKET FORECASTS

Unfortunately, there are no people who can forecast the trend of stock prices correctly at all times. If some few individuals in the past have set better records for accuracy than the great majority of others, their success was probably due as much to chance, luck, or coincidence as to any scientific forecasting ability. Specialized studies made on this point attest to the difficulties of forecasting stock prices, even for the professional experts. For example, the Cowles Commission for Research in Economics published, in 1933, an article entitled "Can Stock Market Forecasters Forecast?" (27) This was supplemented by another study, continuing the theme of the original, published in 1944. (28)* These studies cover the record of forecasters for the 1927–1944 period; in the process of analysis, a total of 6904 professional forecasts was examined. The record showed that the forecasts were many times more bullish than bearish, although more than half the period under review was occupied by bear markets. Evidence pointed to the conclusion that the experts were something less than 50 per cent right in their forecasts and, further, that the records of 11 leading financial periodicals and services since 1927 did not reveal any consistent ability to predict successfully the future course of the stock market. The 1944 Cowles report presents the further evidence that statisticians and economists have achieved only a 33 per cent record of accuracy and that the forecasts of the Dow theory have been correct only 50 per cent of the time. In a similar article on the subject of business forecasting published in *Fortune* magazine for February, 1947, the conclusion was reached that the best forecasters average something less than 55 per cent correctness in calling the turns in the stock market. Since the sensitivity of stock-price fluctuations in the future is not likely to be much different from that in the past, it would seem to follow that the record of future individual forecasters will likely be no more auspicious than that of its predecessors.

* Numbers within parentheses refer to corresponding references in the Bibliography, pp. 181–183.

Cyclical-trend forecasting thus leaves much to be desired, and the game of playing the trend can all too frequently develop into an expensive pastime. In attempting to analyze the trend upon which a prophecy might be supported, market forecasters generally employ one or the other of two methods, and sometimes a combination of both. One method may be referred to as external; the other, internal. The *external* method tries to establish a relationship between the stock-price trend and the business cycle, the presumption being that security-price fluctuations will correspond more or less closely with changes in the general level of business activity. Advocates of this method would study (and try to project into the near-term future) the course of such statistical data as the size of the national income, the Federal Reserve Board Index of Industrial Production, the level of inventories, the amount of retail sales, the movements of commodity prices, the trend of production costs, etc. On the face of it, it would appear that this would be highly logical, for there is considerable historical evidence showing a general correlation between movements in security prices and the level of business activity. Yet it is also not difficult to discover many periods of divergence between the two indices, and even when the movement is somewhat parallel, stock prices, representing the more sensitive index, tend to precede other indices of general business conditions. Evidence is presented in the Frontispiece, particularly for such relatively recent periods as 1952, 1947–1949, and 1940–1942, when stock averages moved in a direction opposite to that in which the United Business Thermometer moved or in a direction not confirmed by the latter's course.

What is needed is an index that is even more sensitive than one of stock prices, one whose movements are more or less regularly and consistently followed by movements in the stock index. Unfortunately, however, no such index yet exists; even if one were developed, its reliability might be open to serious question. To fill the need, it would perhaps be necessary to fashion some sort of index out of a measure of current public psychology, since, at bottom, it is probable that collective hopes and fears are later translated into investment decisions. But a consideration of the many millions of people who are actual or potential investors, as well as the many conflicting psychological crosscurrents that almost daily dominate the market place might well make anyone shrink from the task and despairingly confess its impracticality. In any case, it is reasonably safe to say that business-cycle forecasting is still a very inexact science and that the records of those who use the method to predict stock market trends have not been overly impressive.

To overcome these objections in part, others have attempted to look at the mechanics of the market itself as a basis for a trend forecast, and this we may conveniently identify as the *internal* method. Students of this method feel strongly that the market has an invariable habit of discounting future changes in business activity and that, therefore, to forecast the future of stock prices, one must look at market behavior itself. It is claimed that some inkling of the trading public's expectations for the future can thereby be uncovered. Therefore, study should be made of the movements of price averages, major and intermediate trends, the volume of trading, the kind of buying (investment or speculative, strong or weak), the amount of the short interest, the volume of odd-lot trading, etc. To this end, some financial services have gone to apparently extreme lengths of effort and expense in trying to perfect various elaborately executed statistical models, but their records have not been such that would inspire a great degree of enthusiasm or confidence.

THE DOW THEORY

No discussion of stock market timing would be complete without some reference to the Dow theory and some evaluation of its results. Strictly speaking, the Dow theory attempts to predict major and intermediate turns in the stock market on the basis of a study of the current action of certain price averages in relation to their past movements. From this standpoint, then, the Dow theory could be classified among internal methods of forecasting stock prices. The theory itself is merely a formulation of some principles derived from careful observation of market action in the past. Its early successes brought widespread acclaim, and many enthusiastic followers began to support it almost fanatically. Its acceptance by some and its recognition by others seemed to gain increasing currency in the early 1900's, and in the 1920's and early 1930's it still attracted considerable attention. Since 1937, however, it has increasingly lost popularity, and while it still has its exponents and continues to attract a certain following today, its forecasts no longer seem to be able to retain the fairly widespread docile support it enjoyed in the past. Still, its inclusion seems justified here not only because it is one of the oldest and perhaps most widely known among methods of forecasting stock-price trends, but also because it seems typical of many timing methods that flourished at one time or another in the past when a certain set of conditions prevailed but which inevitably declined in public favor when those conditions changed.

The record of the Dow theory goes back to 1897, when Charles Dow, founder of Dow, Jones & Co., Inc., first evolved the principles of a theory based on the actual market record of the two stock averages that he compiled: the 30-stock Industrial Average and the 20-stock Railroad Average. Dow died in 1902, but his work of interpretation of market trends was carried on by certain disciples such as William P. Hamilton, and more recently, Robert Rhea.

The principal ingredients of the system are as follows:

1. Three types of price fluctuations are recognized: the major trend, the intermediate trend, and the minor or day-to-day movement. The major trend, usually identified with bull or bear markets, might be of one or more years' duration; and the intermediate trend might last one or more months, usually less than one year. The minor movement is generally of little significance except perhaps in helping to define a so-called "line" formation, the outbreak of which would be important in determining the next near-term trend.

2. The Dow-Jones Industrial and Railroad Averages are used jointly for interpretative purposes. Signals of trend change, etc., are

only considered valid if both averages always move more or less together, thus confirming each other's action regularly and consistently.

3. The volume of trading is brought into consideration in trying
to determine when stocks may be overbought or oversold. Thus, as
long as volume is in consonance with the trend of prices (in a bull
market, for instance, increasing volume along with increasing prices
and decreasing volume with decreasing prices) there is no cause
for alarm. But when volume begins to diverge from the price
movement (such as, for instance, decreasing on rallies and increasing on sell-offs), signs should be closely watched for an overbought
condition and a possible vulnerability of prices.

From a trend standpoint, the main interpretative deductions
to be drawn from these ingredients can be listed as follows:

1. A trend will be considered up as long as each successive intermediate fluctuation exceeds the high of the preceding movement
in a sort of wavelike fashion.

2. A downtrend or bear market will exist as long as each successive intermediate fluctuation falls to a point below the low of the
preceding movement.

3. Each major bull or bear trend is presumed to be subject to
interruption from time to time by a temporary change of trend in
the other direction (known as an intermediate trend, or a secondary
reaction). Such a reaction is considered a sort of consolidating
movement useful for correcting the excesses of the preceding phase
of the major trend, and normally might retrace from one-third to
two-thirds of the preceding movement.

4. Major turning points from bull to bear or from bear to bull
are to be recognized from two separate developments:

    a. A divergence of volume from the major price trend.
    b. A pattern of market action that generally takes some
        weeks or months to work itself out but that is character-
        ized by a refusal of prices to go further in the same direc-

tion, up or down, and by one secondary reaction either breaking through the low point of the preceding one (bear-market signal) or exceeding the high point of the preceding one (bull-market signal).

There are perhaps many more details that could be mentioned for more complete understanding, but such at least is the general framework of the theory. It was mentioned above that the system worked fairly well from its early years up to approximately 1937 and that since then the record has not been one to inspire the confidence it attracted earlier.

Why has the Dow theory not performed too well since the late 1930's? One answer may lie in the changing character of the market since that time. Benjamin Graham, in commenting on such market timing methods as the Dow theory, suggests that

. . . as acceptance increases their reliability tends to diminish. This happens for two reasons: First, the passage of time brings new conditions which the old formula no longer fits. Second, in stock market affairs, the popularity of a trading theory has itself an influence on the market's behaviour which detracts in the long run from its profit-making possibilities. (The popularity of the Dow Theory may seem to create its own vindication, since it would make the market advance or decline by the very action of its followers when a buying or selling signal is given. A "stampede" of this kind is, of course, much more of a danger than an advantage to the public trader.) (9)

In the late 1930's and the early 1940's, the movements of the Dow-Jones averages were decidedly erratic and more or less short-lived. When the Dow theory did give a signal, it usually developed that the bulk of the movement was over. Investors who followed the theory sometimes found themselves buying back their securities at prices higher than those at which they had sold them, and sometimes selling their securities at lower prices than those at which they had bought them. Again, in the postwar years, from 1946 through 1949, the market moved in a rather narrow range, and Dow-theory followers frequently found themselves "whipsawed" when they attempted to follow signals that later proved false. Firm believers in the Dow theory must take *some* action whenever a confirmed signal is given. The theory does not brook any hesitation, yet the investor never knows—has no chance of knowing—how much of the move has already been completed by the time the signal is given. If the market happens to be in a narrow range, blind following of the signal can frequently result in sizable losses.

The Dow theory, for most successful results, depends on the amount of the momentum behind a major trend, on how far it will go. If it goes far, and if it is periodically punctuated by secondary reactions that retrace the standard one-third to two-thirds of the preceding movements, the theory might be expected to function reasonably well. Such conditions generally characterized market action before the 1930's. Since then, and since the advent of the Securities and Exchange Commission brought more effective policing and regulation to the stock market, conditions have tended to change.[1] The secondary reaction in a major trend is now almost a thing of the past. Major trends since 1949 seem to follow in almost straight lines before exhausting themselves, and the turn, when it comes, is frequently abrupt and sharp, without the nice and precise patterns that used to provide the Dow theory with its rather unique forecasting ability.

Moreover, critics of the theory have recently begun to question the validity of the requirement that the Railroad Average must confirm the Industrial Average before a real signal can be given. In

[1] The Securities and Exchange Commission, which came into being by act of Congress in 1934, was empowered to regulate security markets in the public interest, and in the pursuance of its mission it removed some major speculative abuses (such as price manipulation, pools, artificial price rigging, bucket shop, etc.) from the operation of national stock exchanges. In addition it was given power to regulate short selling and, in cooperation with the Federal Reserve Board, to control margin trading, which represents the purchase of securities with borrowed money. Appropriate action along these lines tended to make security market trading more investment-minded and less speculative-minded. The over-all effect was to make markets more orderly and quiet and more reflective of real underlying factors of supply and demand. This of course reflected itself in a generally lower volume of trading as well as in narrower monthly ranges of price fluctuation. Again the reader's attention is called to Figure 1 for closer inspection of the monthly price fluctuations of the DJIA for the period 1927–1933 and from 1934 on.

recent years, there have been frequent periods when the two averages pursued divergent trends. When they have moved more or less in consonance, the Railroad Average has sometimes been late in confirming the Industrial Average, thus postponing a valid signal and preventing the purchase of securities at more attractive levels.

Then, too, in any such timing method as the Dow theory, allowance must be made for the loss of current income between the date when a sell signal is given and the subsequent date—perhaps a year later—when a repurchase signal is given. Such a loss of income would be compensated for only if the prices of securities had declined sufficiently to more than offset it. But it would avail the investor little—in fact, it would be likely to produce considerable chagrin—if a buy signal advised the purchase of securities at prices approximately those at which they were sold, with complete loss of current income in between. And if the signal were false—if it were a whipsawing sort of thing—and securities were rebought at higher than their selling prices, one could well have sympathy for the investor who sought another method of market timing.

GROWTH STOCKS

Still the effort to play the trend goes on—the effort to achieve better timing. More recently, the investing public has been urged to buy *growth stocks*. Those who offer this advice realize the many difficulties to be encountered in trying to forecast the trend. They feel that the portfolio of an investor who gets into the right stocks at the right time and holds them long enough will show a substantial profit over several business cycles, due principally to the long-term growth of the companies concerned. All this may be very true, but the nub of the whole problem is this: What are the right stocks and when is the right time? Often, in such an analysis, hindsight may distort sound judgment. It takes no profound intelligence to recognize a growth stock after it has grown, but by that time the chance for additional proportionate future gain may well have passed. To rely on growth stocks, one must recognize and buy the common stock of a growth company before it has started to grow rapidly. Yet if entry of firms into a new industry is not otherwise inhibited or impeded by various special requirements, it is more than likely that the prospective investor will have available for selection a great many small companies that are struggling to get a foothold. This would be the logical time to buy the securities of such companies, since the opportunities for gain are manifestly the greatest; yet as there are many to choose from so also are there many opportunities for loss. Rare indeed is the individual who has the uncanny foresight to select only those companies that will become leaders in their fields in the next generation and to avoid those that will drop by the wayside.

One might well ask: What are the criteria by which a growth stock is recognized? Any growth stock is characterized by a long-term increase in price, based upon a similar increase in company sales, production, assets, earnings, and dividends. To select a growth stock properly, then, it follows that a considerable degree of historical research is necessary. By carefully studying the past patterns of the above six factors, one can pretty well judge the direction of the long-term trend. Of course, growth stocks, like any other group of stocks, will be subject to periodic cyclical fluctuations—the upward trend is not simply a one-way street. But the usual characteristic is that each cyclical low point in the price pattern is above the preceding cyclical low, and each subsequent high point exceeds the preceding cyclical high. Whether the investor cares to indulge in statistical study and is prepared to devote to it the necessary time and effort will largely determine the success of his dealings in growth stocks.

One point regarding growth stocks needs clarification: A growth stock is not necessarily limited to an industry that at any one time may be clothed in the most fashionable robes of romance and glamour, or which may be capturing the maximum popular imagination. The popular impression of a growth stock is that it is one that represents a company producing either a new product or a new line that is on the verge of unlimited expansion. Today, for instance, we hear romantic stories about industries in such fields as plastics, electronics, miracle drugs, petrochemicals, and atomic energy. But the impression given by these stories is not the whole truth. Growth stocks may very well be those of companies that are expanding internally through continuous reinvestment of annual retained earnings as well as those that are expanding externally either vertically or horizontally in their industries through judicious mergers or the purchase of smaller companies, or that may be engaged in extensive research and development programs, or that are developing new technological innovations and new products. But one thing seems to stand out, one thing that all these companies seem to have in common: each can show a proven record of substantial underlying expansion in per-share earnings as well as the prospect for the future of a more rapid expansion of sales and income than can the average corporation.

If we would pursue the growth-stock approach as an alternative to forecasting the cyclical fluctuation, we must not blind ourselves to the problems involved. Not only is there a difficult problem of proper timing, but the problem of selection also is ever present, a problem that has both qualitative and quantitative aspects. As to the proper timing, it is obvious that little can be gained by the average investor if he purchases a growth stock after it has already grown, and after the fact is well-recognized, because then the stock may be selling at a very high price-earnings ratio, may be offering a very low current yield, and may be discounting future earnings years ahead. As to proper selection, it is equally obvious that a very delicate problem in security analysis is involved—a problem that demands a breadth of knowledge, experience, and expert discrimination to which the average investor can not hope to aspire. If the investor limits himself solely to growth stocks, moreover, he may be doing so at the expense of proper and adequate diversification, and thus he may subject his program to too great a concentration of financial risk.

UNDER- AND OVERVALUATON

Some security analysts would prefer to disregard attempts to call the turns in the market as a whole, as defined by some recognized price average, and would favor directing attention toward individual stocks with the objective of discovering situations where clear under- or overvaluation seems to exist. They, too, would be skeptical of trend forecasting as a method for achieving good timing; their good timing would come from buying certain stocks when they are cheap or undervalued, and selling them when they are dear or overvalued. An operation such as this has the advantage of providing continuous opportunity for study and research by the investor, as well as more or less continuous commitment of funds, because attention is focused on individual stocks and not on the general market. All stocks do not necessarily move together. Thus, situations of over- and undervaluation can normally be expected at all levels of the market; even when the market is at a high level, some stocks may be undervalued, and when the market is at a low level, some stocks may still be overvalued. Attempting to call and follow turns in the market as a whole, on the other hand, may lead to perplexing periods when one is out of stocks entirely for a year or more while the averages are working out their price pattern, especially if the stocks one may have sold should be describing a pattern that is counter to that of the averages.

The concept of under- and overvaluation, however, necessarily implies some *normal* or *intrinsic* value that corresponds to what a stock is currently worth on the basis of recognized principles of valuation. This would be the value or level around which the price of the stock would tend to fluctuate. If the analyst could then discover situations where the current price is substantially below intrinsic value, he would single them out as candidates for purchase. Conversely, where a stock was priced well above its intrinsic value, he would probably mark it as one suitable for sale or a short position.

This all sounds very well and appears very simple. But this

method of timing, while it may have merit, is still a rather difficult approach.[2] It involves tools of analysis in the determination of an intrinsic value that can be efficiently employed only by experts. Moreover, the interpretation of results and the discriminating appraisal of valuations—and these are most important—present problems to which the average investor with his limited breadth of knowledge and experience can not hope to find a complete solution. Analytical tools such as expected future earnings, expected future dividends, capitalization rates of such earnings and dividends, and intelligent appraisal of asset values are not those that can be entrusted to the inexpert investor.

The valuation approach, while applying more particularly to the proper timing of purchase and sale of individual stocks, has also been developed to the extent of determining a normal or intrinsic value for a group of stocks, such as the Dow-Jones Industrial Average. Such an intrinsic value, it is suggested by the analysts who favor the method, could be used to establish a trend line on the basis of which a variable-ratio buying-and-selling schedule could be determined for the operation of a particular type of formula plan. The details of such timing systems will be discussed in Chapter 4.

THE THEORY OF CONTRARY OPINION

Another approach to the timing problem derives its support from the observation that, in past major market turns, the majority of the speculating public has always been wrong. The tops of bull markets are generally characterized by heavy public participation, and the bottoms of bear markets by the absence of public activity. The theory of contrary opinion is essentially founded on the understandable principle that, if the few are to be right, the many must be wrong. As stock prices rise, more and more people be-

[2] This assumes, of course, that it would be difficult for the individual investor to attempt to approach the problem by himself. His difficulty in this respect might be overcome by his subscription to a professional service which would advise him periodically. The success of his program, then, would be predicated upon the degree of competency of the advice received.

come interested, but their interest invariably does not become acute until the final explosive phase of the rise has been reached. Strictly speaking, this explosive phase is the direct result of the unintelligent scramble of the public to buy stocks for quick speculative gain, influenced by the rampant emotionalism of the times. People are goaded into action by rumor and gossip of all sorts, by the speculative urge to gamble, by an unreasoning attitude about the continued duration of the rise. At such times the smart trader will be only too happy to give the public the stocks it wants to buy. At the bottom of bear markets, on the other hand, a wave of painful disillusionment sweeps over the public. As prices fall, the public becomes panic-stricken and sells at prices far below true value, again because of the prevailing fear and pessimism, and by the time that prices hover around a bottom, the public is usually completely out of the market, having sold or having been forced to sell at substantial losses. It is at precisely such times that the smart trader— the minority—will be only too happy to buy the stocks that the public has been stampeding to get rid of.

Followers of this theory try to study certain factors which they say reflect public market participation. Principal among the factors that are carefully studied are the volume of odd-lot trading, unusual activity or inactivity in low-priced speculative stocks, the relative volume of brokers' loans, and the strength or weakness of so-called "blue chip" stocks in relation to the general market. There is much to be said for this method of timing, and, as we shall see in subsequent chapters, formula plans as a whole constitute a timing device that essentially reflects the theory of contrary opinion. In fact, one of the primary features of formula plans is the attempt to divorce the investor from his emotions and to force him to do things that run counter to the prevailing investment psychology. In this lies the basis for the potential growth attainable under formula-plan operation. But the major criticism of the contrary-opinion theory is that it is difficult to determine precisely when public participation *is* at its maximum and when at its minimum. Public interest generally runs in waves of optimism and waves of pessimism. The speculator would try to detect the one point at which he feels public interest is

at its most irrational level—its highest or lowest pitch, so to speak—
and at that point he would be influenced to dispose of all his stocks
or to repurchase them as the case might be. But unfortunately, that
point might not be the high or the low that the price movement
finally reached. Formula plans, on the other hand, try to allow for
this difficulty. They recognize the impossibility of consistently calling
the exact highs and lows. They try to perfect a compromise with the
contrary-opinion theory by working it out on a gradual or scale
basis. They provide for disposal of their common stocks in previously determined proportions whenever stock prices exceed a certain average level, and for reaccumulation of stocks in easy stages
whenever their prices fall below such level. The following chapters
will explore the implications of this orderly, timed method of investing.

Chapter 2

The Formula-Plan Approach to the Timing Problem

FUNDAMENTAL PRESUMPTIONS

The preceding chapter indicated certain approaches to the problem of timing and pointed out that preoccupation with trend forecasting can frequently lead to unfortunate results. Moreover, an attempt either to pick growth stocks or to do the opposite of what the public is doing can obviously involve certain hazards.

The question, then, is whether there is an approach to the crucial problem of timing that can provide the investor with more peace of mind. One possibility is the formula plan. In the preceding chapter, in discussing the need for diversification in planning an investment program, four major principles were laid down, principles that, over the years, have achieved general recognition among security analysts as guides to sound investing. It is pertinent at this time to offer a fifth principle: diversification in the time of purchase and sale; in due course, this principle may receive sufficient acceptance to be included in the same category as the other four.

The formula method may be classified as another kind of diversification, for it implies a diversity of prices for buying and selling stocks: stocks are not all bought or sold at the same time or at the same price. If prices are declining, the formula-plan manager diversifies his purchase price by increasing his commitments on a scaledown (thereby lowering average costs); if prices are rising, he disposes of his stocks at increasingly higher prices above average costs. The direction of the price movement is immaterial to his plan of operation; what *is* material is that stock prices continue to fluctuate. His price interest centers on the *degree* of fluctuation; not only is the whole framework of his plan closely geared to price changes, but also, the more the fluctuation, the better are his chances for ultimately satisfactory results.

Basically, then, the formula approach encompasses methods of investment timing that require more or less automatic sales of stocks above their cost levels when prices rise and more or less automatic purchases below their previous selling levels when prices fall. In effect, its purpose is to require action that apparently runs counter to the currently existing trend of the market. The formula planner will be selling when the intensity of public buying is pushing prices up and he will be buying when the intensity of public selling is forcing prices down. It is a well-established fact that the public, in its response to mass psychology with its recurring waves of overoptimism and overpessimism, is usually wrong in its speculative commitments. When the public is in a buying mood, it carries stock prices far above what later proves to be the worth of the stocks; when it is in a selling mood, it forces prices down to levels substantially below long-run values.

In the course of these fluctuations, the public generally gets hurt. Only the astute or lucky minority of investors and speculators (and this includes large institutional funds, the big individual operators, and professional traders) ever gets out of stocks at or near market tops or gets in at or near market bottoms. The formula planner, by the very nature of his method, plans his operations so that there is a certain measure of similarity to the action of the minority. He may not maximize his gain to the extent the nimble and successful speculator does—because he does not attempt to detect the exact top and bottom—but he tries to take periodic advantage of abnormal market conditions brought about by the public's alternate expression of overconfidence on the one hand and unwarranted pessimism on the other.

This is precisely where formula planning meets one of the greatest tests of investing, for the whole idea is based on the following four fundamental presumptions.

PRESUMPTION 1

The first presumption is that stock prices will continue to fluctuate; that an up- or downtrend will inevitably be succeeded by a reversal of the movement; and that, if purchases are made on a scale-down or sales on a scale-up, profits should accrue whenever the market trend reverses itself to an extent comparable to that of the preceding movement.[1] Of course, profits could be maximized under formula-plan operation if stock-price fluctuations were perfectly symmetrical both in amplitude and duration. However, since such a pattern has not been characteristic of past fluctuations, and since it is not likely to be characteristic of the future either, symmetry of price fluctuation is not a necessary implication under Presumption 1.

PRESUMPTION 2

The second presumption is that the individual securities that comprise the stock portion of the formula-plan portfolio will tend to move in close correlation to the movements of the whole stock market, or to some widely recognized index of the whole market such as the Dow-Jones Industrial Average (DJIA). A great many formula plans, particularly those of the *variable-ratio* type, adopt the DJIA as the index upon which their buying-and-selling schedules are based. Thus, if the DJIA rises and reaches a point calling for the sale of some stocks, it must be presumed that the individual

---

[1] The fluctuation referred to is the short-term or cyclical variety, the type that is associated with the business cycle. The methods of forecasting the longer term or secular trend will be dealt with more fully in Chapters 4 and 8.

stocks to be sold have also advanced in more or less equal proportion to the rise in the DJIA. If this were not so—if the stocks to be sold had, perhaps, declined in price rather than advanced—execution of the sell signal would result in a significant loss and the whole formula idea would be discredited. However, it was pointed out earlier that formula plans are primarily timing devices, not stock-selection devices; and if such a loss situation should develop, it would be the fault not of the formula plan itself but of the methods used in the original stock selection. Much of the danger involved in certain stocks that pursue price patterns of their own can be overcome if a more conservative stock-selection policy is adopted. For instance, the formula planner might limit himself to the 30 stocks that comprise the DJIA itself, thus insuring a comparable movement; or he might restrict himself to certain other blue chips or "light blue chips" that have long and successful records of earnings and dividends and that also have past price records of considerable volatility. Of course, profits might be maximized if one would concentrate on stocks such as high-leverage situations[2] or those which consistently in the past have outperformed the DJIA on both the upside and downside; but it should also be pointed out that such a preference might possibly entail a greater degree of speculative risk.

PRESUMPTION 3

The third presumption is that stocks, when bought under a formula plan on a scale-down, do not ultimately become worthless or else decline to a nominal level from which no appreciable recovery takes place. Many instances could be cited of stocks that went down in price and did not come back for years, or did not recover at all because the companies failed. However, this is primarily a matter of stock selection and not a timing factor that would be encompassed by a formula plan. The problem of proper

[2] A high-leverage common stock is one which is preceded in the capitalization by a heavy amount of prior claims to earnings and assets, such as bonds and preferred stocks.

stock selection is equally acute with any system of market operation or any method of market timing. This much, however, can be said in favor of the formula-plan method: By removing the element of timing as a major factor demanding his continuous attention, the investor can devote correspondingly more time to security analysis and to the discriminating process of selecting the particular stocks that promise best to satisfy his needs and requirements.

It would be possible to overcome the selection problem by confining purchases to the older, better-known stocks, either those in the DJIA or those that have good quality ratings and long records of earnings and dividends. The only danger that all stocks, good as well as bad, might become worthless at some time in the future consists in the overthrow of our capitalistic system and all the institutions upon which it is based. Such an eventuality, it is believed, is not a reasonable likelihood.

Presumption 4

The final presumption is that, when stock prices are undergoing violent swings, it is practically impossible for the average individual to disassociate emotion from sound judgment. When emotions run rampant, everyone tends to get overly bullish or overly bearish, and when one allows his feelings and his current psychology to guide his market actions, distressing results usually follow. When pessimism is everywhere, people are in a selling mood, precisely when they should be buying; when optimism rules, people jump in to buy anything and everything at fantastic prices, precisely when they should be selling. The formula investor, if he adheres rigidly to his timing schedule, is constrained to do things that are the opposite of those impelled by general emotions; he reduces his stocks when bullishness prevails and he increases them when bearishness prevails. If emotion does not substantially enter into his calculations, the soundness of his investment decisions is enhanced. Rather than be moved to rash and ill-considered action by the influence of current mass psychology, he is in a position to profit by it.

THE GENERAL NATURE OF FORMULA PLANS

The individual formula plans that are separately analyzed in succeeding chapters have in common three features that are discussed in the sections that follow.

AGGRESSIVE AND DEFENSIVE PORTIONS

All formula plans provide for the division of the capital fund into two broad parts. One part is called *aggressive;* the other part, *defensive.* Aggressive securities are those, chiefly common stocks, which allow for some speculative play and provide sensitivity to price fluctuation. Strictly speaking, an aggressive security may be any type of issue that is subject to fairly wide price swings in its response to changing economic conditions. In accordance with this general description, some formula plans include in their aggressive portion certain issues such as low-grade, non-dividend-paying preferred stocks and defaulted bonds. But the bulk of the aggressive portion will normally consist of common stocks. Because common stocks represent, essentially, the residual element in entitlement to earnings, dividends, and assets, their market prices tend to fluctuate in accordance with basic fluctuations in the residual entitlement.

The defensive part of the fund is more conservative in nature, designed to provide assets that are less subject to price fluctuation. The safest of such assets is cash itself, and some formula plans provide for keeping the defensive portion entirely in cash at all times. However, the defensive part of the fund often assumes major proportions in relation to the total, and, if large amounts of cash were held for long periods, the total fund might be sadly lacking in current income.

Substantially the same results in minimizing fluctuation of principal can be achieved without loss of income if the defensive portion is consistently invested in high-grade securities such as United States government long-term bonds or private-corporation bonds of very high quality. Some formula plans permit part of the defensive portion to be invested in high-grade investment-type preferred stocks that are currently paying their prescribed dividend rates and have done so consistently in the past.

The main objective to be achieved in the management of the defensive fund is stability of principal. Essentially, the defensive portion must be thought of as a primary reserve into which the proceeds of the sales of aggressive securities are placed periodically for so-called safekeeping and for protection of realized profits. Similarly, it is the reserve from which funds are drawn gradually as stock prices decline to levels that call for automatic purchases under the pre-established buying-and-selling schedule. As stock prices rise, aggressive securities are gradually reduced. Presumably, profits are realized, and they are added to the defensive portion, which theoretically immobilizes them or at least retains their dollar amounts intact. (By definition, the defensive portion is not subject to much price fluctuation, come what may.)

As stock prices fall, on the other hand, the principal of the defensive portion is periodically drawn upon to provide funds with which to repurchase the aggressive securities that, presumably, were sold at higher prices in the preceding phase of the cycle and may now be approaching "bargain counter" levels. Thus, at any one time, the defensive portion of the fund may include a variety of assets—a part may be in cash, a part in United States Government bonds, a part in high-grade corporate bonds, and a part in investment-type preferred stocks. The ideal policy in the management of the defensive portion is maximum current yield consistent with maximum stability of principal. To achieve the most successful results from this policy, the formula-plan manager definitely cannot afford to neglect his defensive securities; they, like the aggressive securities, deserve constant attention and study.

Some idea can now be had of the potential long-term growth inherent in formula-plan operation. As one stock-price cycle succeeds another, the total fund should gradually increase, assuming that capital gains are retained in the fund for reinvestment. As profits are realized on stocks during the upswing in one cycle, a greater fund is automatically made available for purchase on the succeeding downswing, because not only is the original principal available for reinvestment in stocks but the amount of any realized profit is also available. Such is the ideal operation of formula plans. However, the extent of approach to the ideal depends in large part upon the type of formula plan adopted, the manner of stock and bond selection, the method used in the determination of the long-term trend, and the accuracy of the buying-and-selling schedule. If these are good, satisfactory results will likely be achieved; if they are poor, results may be disappointing. These matters will be further evaluated in Chapter 8.

BUYING AND SELLING POINTS

All formula plans involve establishment in advance of certain rules that govern automatic purchases and sales of aggressive securities as conditions warrant, or more properly, automatic transfers from stocks to bonds and from bonds to stocks, as selling or buying points respectively are reached according to the formula schedule. Usually, certain proportions of the fund—as between stocks and bonds—are predetermined in accordance with some normal or average level of stock prices. As prices rise, some proportion of the aggressive fund is sold and the proceeds are added to the defensive fund. As prices fall, the aggressive fund is gradually built up by selling some proportion of the defensive fund. These systematic rules for proportionate changes constitute the core of all formula plans; the essential difference between one type of plan and another lies in the varying nature of the rules.

All formula plans fall into two major categories: the equalization type and the variable-ratio type. Equalization plans can be further classified as constant-ratio or constant-dollar plans. The former involves the continuous maintenance of a predetermined *percentage of the fund* and the latter a predetermined *dollar amount* in stocks. As stock prices fluctuate after the inauguration of either plan, transfers between stocks and bonds take place only to the extent necessary to restore the fund to its original, predetermined investment distribution. No matter whether the market is high or low, only a sufficient amount of stocks is sold or bought to re-establish the originally determined aggressive percentage or dollar amount.

Variable-ratio plans, on the other hand, seek to establish different stock/bond ratios in accordance with general market fluctuations. When market levels are considered high, only a minimum proportion of the fund will be retained in stocks; when market levels are considered low, a maximum proportion will be built up in stocks. In some cases, no stocks at all will be retained; in some cases the fund may become entirely aggressive. By their very nature, variable-ratio plans are more complicated than are those of the equalization type and they permit a wide variety of operational details.

The basic differences between these various types of plans will be analyzed thoroughly in later chapters. It will suffice at this point to note the five major ways in which the plans differ:

1. The proportions of the total fund which will be held in stocks and bonds at different market levels.

2. The methods of determining buying-and-selling schedules, including establishment of suitable average levels of prices.

3. The selection of an appropriate price index, the fluctuation of which will establish transfer or action points.

4. The number or frequency of transfer points considered desirable and the amounts to be transferred at such points.

5. The methods employed in appraising the range of future stock-price fluctuation—that is, determining what is a relatively high market level at which a minimum proportion will be held in stocks, and what is a relatively low market level at which a maximum proportion will be held in stocks.

ELIMINATION OF FORECASTS

All formula plans are supposed to eliminate price forecasting as much as possible—forecasting, that is, of the *near-term* or *cyclical* variety.[3] They rest on the assumption that stock prices *will* fluctuate in more or less rhythmic cyclical sequence; they are designed to take some advantage of *any* movement, whether it is up or down.

However, to say that formula plans try to avoid the necessity of cyclical-price forecasting is not to say that no assumptions at all concerning future market action are permissible. Certain assumptions of a *secular* nature—a fairly long-term viewpoint—are necessarily involved in the very basis upon which formula plans are established. In order to predetermine rules for shifting from aggressive to defensive and vice versa, there must be some general assumption concerning the direction and the degree of ascent or descent of the long-term price trend, as well as the range within which the market will fluctuate in the future. This is not necessarily so true of the equalization plans but it is a matter of particular importance to the variable-ratio plans. To assume, for instance, that the DJIA will move within the range of 500–200 for the next 10 years is a far different thing from saying that the Average will rise or fall by 25 points in the next 3 months. Thus, it is possible to generalize by saying that price forecasts of the immediate future—those of only short-term validity—have no place in typical formula-plan operation.

[3] Whether or not all price forecasting, even of an intermediate nature, can be eliminated is a debatable issue. The problem is discussed in greater detail in Chapter 8.

Equalization Plans

We have examined some of the general features and fundamental assumptions upon which all formula plans are based and we may now proceed to an analysis and evaluation of specific plans. As noted in Chapter 3, formula plans can be classified as the equalization type considered in this chapter or as the variable-ratio type considered in Chapter 4.

It is necessary, first of all, to define more precisely what is meant by equalization plans. Such plans, of course, basically provide for the separation of an investment fund into two parts: an aggressive part devoted to securities (generally, common stocks) that are presumed to fluctuate in price rather consistently and a defensive part devoted to securities (generally, high-grade bonds) that are presumed to be fairly stable in market value. The cardinal feature of these plans is that they require, at periodic intervals, an evening-up or equalizing of the aggressive and defensive portions of the fund.

Usually such plans start out with a fund evenly divided between stocks and bonds, although, it should be pointed out, this is not a necessary requirement. The bond portion, for purposes of analysis, is presumed to be fixed in market value—that is, free from any price fluctuation. Only the stock portion is presumed to fluctuate. As the stock portion moves up or down in market value, after the establishment of the initial position, enough stocks are sold or bought to bring about a restoration of the two portions of the fund to the predetermined original position. When stocks are sold, the proceeds are added to the bond portion of the fund and are immediately reinvested in securities of a defensive nature. When stocks are bought, the funds for the required amount of purchase are made available through the sale of some part of the bond account.

This is the over-all plan of operation. All equalization plans call for taking profits as stock prices advance or purchasing additional shares as stock prices decline, so lowering average cost. But, upon the initiation of such a plan, differences arise over the proper method of establishing and subsequently maintaining the stock and bond portions of the fund. One school of thought prefers a definite, fixed sum of dollar market value to represent the stock portion. Subsequent changes are made to restore or maintain the preset, fixed dollar value. This method is referred to as the *constant-dollar plan.* Another school of thought prefers a definite fixed percentage of the total fund to represent the stock portion. Subsequent changes are made to restore the preset fixed percentage. This method is referred to as the *constant-ratio plan.* The following sections consider these two plans in detail.

CONSTANT-DOLLAR PLAN

The constant-dollar plan has often been recommended to the average investor for its extreme simplicity. It works like this: At the start, a decision is made on the number of dollars to be committed to the aggressive portion of the fund; the balance is then committed to the defensive portion. To inaugurate the plan, both dollar sums are invested in their respective types of securities. Also, it is determined in advance that changes between stocks and bonds will be made, as conditions warrant, *only* for the purpose of restoring the aggressive portion to its original dollar value.

Assume, for an example, that the plan is started with a fund of

$50,000 and it is decided that $25,000 will consist of aggressive securities. Then, if stock prices rise and the aggressive portion increases to, say $30,000, $5000 of stocks will be sold and the proceeds reinvested in bonds, and thus the preset dollar sum will be
re-established. The two portions of the fund would then be as
follows:

	STOCKS	BONDS	TOTAL FUND
Before transfer	$30,000	$25,000	$55,000
After transfer	25,000	30,000	55,000

Conversely, if the aggressive portion declines to, say, $15,000,
then $10,000 of bonds will be sold and the proceeds reinvested in
stocks, thus bringing the stock portion back to the original dollar figure. The two portions of the fund would then stand as follows:

	STOCKS	BONDS	TOTAL FUND
Before transfer	$15,000	$25,000	$40,000
After transfer	25,000	15,000	40,000

All this looks simple enough on the surface. But this major question naturally arises: How are the points of transfer from bonds to
stocks or stocks to bonds determined? To allow such decisions to
rest solely on the judgment of the investor and perhaps also on his
emotions, whims, and fancies might lead to overtrading in the stock
section, with attendant frequency of brokerage commissions and
perhaps odd-lot fees. Such additional costs might nullify much of
the gain and thus tend to defeat the basic purpose of the plan itself.
One approach to this problem would be to limit such changes between the two portions of the fund to a specified time interval, such
as once every six months or once every year. Although this would
tend to overcome the objection against overtrading, how is one to
know that the time interval specified for revision would be the one
most profitable for the fund? The major part of the fluctuation in
stock prices may have taken place between two revision points, and
thus the best opportunities to buy or sell stocks may well have been
forgone.

To meet this situation, it is preferable to base transfer points upon some percentage change in market price. This may be accomplished in either of two ways:

1. By restoring the value of the aggressive portion to the preset dollar sum whenever a certain percentage change has occurred in some well-recognized average of stock prices. The usual market average selected is the DJIA, and the usual change calling for a transfer is 10 per cent.

2. By restoring the fixed dollar sum whenever the stock portion of the fund changes by a certain percentage. The determination of this percentage is open to somewhat more discretion than is that of the percentage change in (1), for it depends on the preferences and requirements of the individual concerned. A usual arrangement is to take some action whenever the stock portion advances or declines 20 per cent from the preset dollar sum.

Table 1 presents a hypothetical example that illustrates how the constant-dollar plan would operate with transfer points based upon a 10 per cent advance or decline in the DJIA. For simplicity, a number of assumptions were made. The starting point of the Average was taken as 400, with subsequent 10 per cent price movements carrying it above and below that point. The final movement returns the Average to 400 and so completes the price cycle. It was further assumed that the aggressive portion would fluctuate in exact proportion to the market average—an unrealistic assumption that is excused only by the need for a lucid presentation of the principle. A final assumption was that defensive securities are not affected by changes in general market levels. The reader is cautioned that the fluctuations used in the table have no correspondence with reality— the DJIA does not move with such obliging regularity.

Over a complete market cycle, the constant-dollar plan will, under the assumed conditions, provide a profit. It should be observed that the $1100 increase in the total size of the hypothetical fund at Period 11 of Table 1 represents capital appreciation only. To measure the real productivity, or average annual return, from such a plan, the annual dividend and interest return from the two portions of the account must be added to the realized annual capital gain. The amount of dividends and interest would vary from year to year, depending on the size and frequency of stock-bond transfers, but it should not be difficult to net, over a period of years, an average annual return of approximately 7 or 8 per cent.

TABLE 1.   CONSTANT-DOLLAR PLAN

(A hypothetical example based on a $50,000 portfolio; aggressive securities equal $25,000)

PERIOD	CHANGES IN PORTFOLIO*	DEFENSIVE PORTION	AGGRESSIVE PORTION	TOTAL VALUE OF PORTFOLIO
1	DJIA at 400 (starting point)	$25,000	$25,000	$50,000
2	DJIA advances to 440	25,000	27,500	52,500
	Sell aggressive and buy defensive securities	27,500	25,000	52,500
3	DJIA advances to 484	27,500	27,500	55,000
	Sell aggressive and buy defensive securities	30,000	25,000	55,000
4	DJIA advances to 532	30,000	27,500	57,500
	Sell aggressive and buy defensive securities	32,500	25,000	57,500
5	DJIA declines to 480	32,500	22,500	55,000
	Sell defensive and buy aggressive securities	30,000	25,000	55,000
6	DJIA declines to 432	30,000	22,500	52,500
	Sell defensive and buy aggressive securities	27,500	25,000	52,500
7	DJIA declines to 388	27,500	22,500	50,000
	Sell defensive and buy aggressive securities	25,000	25,000	50,000
8	DJIA declines to 350	25,000	22,500	47,500
	Sell defensive and buy aggressive securities	22,500	25,000	47,500
9	DJIA advances to 385	22,500	27,500	50,000
	Sell aggressive and buy defensive securities	25,000	25,000	50,000
10	DJIA advances to 424	25,000	27,500	52,500
	Sell aggressive and buy defensive securities	27,500	25,000	52,500
11	DJIA declines 5.6% to 400	27,500	23,600	51,100

* Adjusted for every 10 per cent advance or decline in DJIA from previous level.

Because of its dollar-averaging aspects as successive purchases are made on the way down, the original size of the fund will be restored at a price level below that at the start, assuming a downtrend in prices followed by a recovery. For example, in Period 9 of Table 1, the total size of the fund is $50,000 at a price level of 385, whereas the original fund had the same dollar amount when the price level was at 400. In addition, this type of plan is easy to set up, simple to operate, and easy to understand.

But extreme simplicity may be an advantage of somewhat dubious merit, and this plan has therefore lent itself to criticism along certain lines. In the first place, the stock portion of the fund never grows in absolute dollar amount. The same predetermined stock/bond relationship is maintained, regardless of changes in stock prices. Therefore, capital gain is never maximized, for to do so would require increasing the dollar amount of the stock portion as prices decline, and decreasing the dollar amount as prices rise. The long-term profit possibilities of the constant-dollar plan are therefore definitely limited. Secondly, the plan is not well adapted to withstand protracted and severe movements in stock prices, either upward or downward. If a long decline takes place, the defensive portion might well be exhausted before the decline stops, and the fund would then become immobilized. This is illustrated in Table 2, which is based on the assumptions of a 10 per cent movement in the DJIA and a 20 per cent change in stock/bond portions. To make Tables 1 and 2 comparable, the same price level for the DJIA as in Table 1 is taken as the starting point. If the Average should continue to decline below 237 no further action could be taken, other than a little switching from one common stock to another. As a result, many favorable opportunities to accumulate additional shares at lower prices would have to be forgone.

Similarly, it can be demonstrated that, as conditions become most favorable for realizing capital gains with a rise in prices (particularly over a long term), the constant-dollar plan becomes most restricted in capitalizing on the opportunity. This is true because, at each transfer point, the entire amount of the profit is transferred to

TABLE 2.   CONSTANT-DOLLAR FUND

(*Hypothetical exhaustion in an assumed price decline*)

DJIA	ACTION	STOCKS	BONDS	TOTAL FUND
400		$25,000	$25,000	$50,000
360		20,000	25,000	45,000
	Sell $5000 bonds;			
	buy $5000 stocks	25,000	20,000	45,000
324		20,000	20,000	40,000
	Sell $5000 bonds;			
	buy $5000 stocks	25,000	15,000	40,000
292		20,000	15,000	35,000
	Sell $5000 bonds;			
	buy $5000 stocks	25,000	10,000	35,000
263		20,000	10,000	30,000
	Sell $5000 bonds;			
	buy $5000 stocks	25,000	5,000	30,000
237		20,000	5,000	25,000
	Sell $5000 bonds;			
	buy $5000 stocks	25,000	0	25,000

the defensive fund, and thus the aggressive portion becomes a smaller and smaller percentage of the total fund. The process is illustrated in Table 3, in which the price range of the DJIA in Table 2 is reversed. It is assumed that each 11 per cent advance in the Average will establish a transfer point and that a similar 20 per cent change in the stock/bond portions will be made.

Moreover, even without a long-term rise in price, the stock portion would become a smaller and smaller percentage of the total fund as the plan operated successfully. As more and more profit was transferred at each action point to the defensive portion, the larger the latter would become in relation to the total fund. If a plan were started originally with one-half of the dollar fund in stocks, such one-half could, after a series of profitable transfers, gradually shrink to perhaps 30 or even 20 per cent of the total. The question would then be whether to increase the dollar amount in stocks in order that the original 50/50 stock/bond relationship could be reestablished. Probably this would be desirable from the standpoint of more profitable long-term operation. The adjustment could be accomplished whenever the stock portion declined to, say, 30 or 35

TABLE 3. CONSTANT-DOLLAR FUND

(*Hypothetical dilution of aggressive portion in an assumed price rise*)

DJIA	ACTION	STOCKS	BONDS	TOTAL FUND	STOCK/BOND RATIO
237		$25,000	$25,000	$50,000	50/50
263		30,000	25,000	55,000	
	Sell $5000 stocks; buy $5000 bonds	25,000	30,000	55,000	46/54
292		30,000	30,000	60,000	
	Sell $5000 stocks; buy $5000 bonds	25,000	35,000	60,000	42/58
324		30,000	35,000	65,000	
	Sell $5000 stocks; buy $5000 bonds	25,000	40,000	65,000	38/62
360		30,000	40,000	70,000	
	Sell $5000 stocks; buy $5000 bonds	25,000	45,000	70,000	36/54
400		30,000	45,000	75,000	
	Sell $5000 stocks; buy $5000 bonds	25,000	50,000	75,000	33/67

per cent of the total, and would be so timed that the actual equalizing operation would take place only when a transfer point which required a purchase, not a sale, of stocks was reached.

Bearing these limitations in mind, the constant-dollar plan may appeal to investors who prefer a simple, easy-to-operate formula that involves a minimum of calculation and computation. The plan seems to work best when stock prices fluctuate moderately in each direction from a trend line, with an alternate deviation of a more or less regular percentage. It probably works best with a starting fund evenly divided between stocks and bonds if the level of stock prices is neither historically high nor historically low. If either of the latter conditions prevails, then the success of the plan will largely hinge upon the judgment and discretion exercised in determining the original proportions, more dollars being allocated to the stock fund when the level of stock prices is thought to be historically low and less when the level is thought to be historically high. This point is evaluated in Chapter 8.

CONSTANT-RATIO PLAN

Instead of a fixed sum of dollars for the aggressive portion, the constant-ratio plan allocates a *fixed percentage* of the fund to stocks. At periodic intervals, the total portfolio is revalued, percentages are determined, and readjustments are made in the aggressive portion to restore the fixed percentage originally established. Table 4 illustrates, by a hypothetical example, how the constant-ratio idea works. To facilitate comparison, the same basic assumptions of Table 1 govern the construction of Table 4. As in the constant-dollar case, an original fund of $50,000 is assumed. Initially, the fund is evenly divided between stocks and bonds, and, at the starting point, both plans are identical. However, as soon as prices begin to fluctuate, divergences between the two begin to appear. At Period 2, after an assumed 10 per cent rise in the Average and in the aggressive portion of the fund, the total fund stands at $52,500 and some action is called for. Instead of transferring to the defensive portion all of the dollar gain, only one-half is so transferred, so that the two portions are restored to their original relationship. As each successive action point is reached, the two portions are again totaled and the increase or decrease in the fund is noted. (Since it is assumed that the bond portion does not fluctuate, the entire change is in the stock portion.)

If the fund has increased, stocks equal in dollar value to *one-half* of the increase are sold and the proceeds are reinvested in defensive securities. If the fund has decreased, bonds equal in dollar value to one-half of the decrease are sold and the proceeds are reinvested in stocks.

Aside from a fundamentally different approach to the method by which the two portions of the fund are periodically equalized, there is no significant difference between the constant-dollar and constant-ratio plans in the mechanics of their operation. As is true of the constant-dollar approach, the constant-ratio plan must provide a desirable basis for transfer. The transfer point may be related to some percentage movement in, say, the DJIA or to the percentage

TABLE 4. CONSTANT-RATIO PLAN

*(A hypothetical example based on a $50,000 portfolio; aggressive
securities equal 50 per cent of portfolio)*

PERIOD	CHANGES IN PORTFOLIO*	DEFENSIVE PORTION	AGGRESSIVE PORTION	TOTAL VALUE OF PORTFOLIO
1	DJIA at 400 (starting point)	$25,000	$25,000	$50,000
2	DJIA advances to 440	25,000	27,500	52,500
	Sell aggressive and buy defensive securities to equalize the portions	26,250	26,250	52,500
3	DJIA advances to 484	26,250	28,875	55,125
	Sell aggressive and buy defensive securities to equalize the portions	27,562	27,563	55,125
4	DJIA advances to 532	27,562	30,319	57,881
	Sell aggressive and buy defensive securities to equalize the portions	28,940	28,941	57,881
5	DJIA declines to 480	28,940	26,047	54,987
	Sell defensive and buy aggressive securities to equalize the portions	27,493	27,494	54,987
6	DJIA declines to 432	27,493	24,745	52,238
	Sell defensive and buy aggressive securities to equalize the portions	26,119	26,119	52,238
7	DJIA declines to 388	26,119	23,507	49,626
	Sell defensive and buy aggressive securities to equalize the portions	24,813	24,813	49,626
8	DJIA declines to 350	24,813	22,332	47,145
	Sell defensive and buy aggressive securities to equalize the portions	23,572	23,573	47,145
9	DJIA advances to 385	23,572	25,930	49,502
	Sell aggressive and buy defensive securities to equalize the portions	24,751	24,751	49,502
10	DJIA advances to 424	24,751	27,226	51,977
	Sell aggressive and buy defensive securities to equalize the portions	25,988	25,989	51,977
11	DJIA declines 5.6% to 400	25,988	24,534	50,522

* Adjusted for every 10 per cent advance or decline in DJIA from previous level.

movements of the stock and bond portions relative to the total fund. Thus, if a 50/50 position were the starting point, transfers might take place whenever the stock portion appreciated to, say, 60 per cent of the total or depreciated to, say, 40 per cent of the total. Such a procedure would require that the investor be willing to revalue his holdings periodically so that no potential transfer points were missed. Perhaps a desirable criterion might be a determination of percentages at intervals of 3 or 6 months, intervals that are long enough to avoid unnecessary computation and short enough to avoid missing any major or sudden movement in stock prices. But whenever transfer points are based upon changes in the relative proportions of the two parts of the fund, many valuations—daily ones, conceivably—might be required as a sale or purchase point was approached. The possibility might be considered a disadvantage of this method of determining transfer points but, of course, a lot depends on the nature and enthusiasm of the individual investor. Substantially the same results could be achieved, though, by basing transfer points on certain percentage movements in the DJIA, combined with a periodic review of the fund every 3 or 6 months.

Another problem that the investor who uses a constant-ratio plan must solve is the distribution of the fund between stocks and bonds at the starting point. The answer to this will depend on the relative conservatism of the investor and on his preference or need for capital gain and higher yield. If he prefers a larger capital gain or a higher yield, and if he is prepared to undertake a somewhat greater degree of risk, he might establish an initial 65/35 or 60/40 stock/bond ratio. If, on the other hand, he is essentially conservative and prefers the more stable but lower yield from fixed-income securities, his initial stock/bond ratio might be 40/60 or 35/65. The fund with the greater portion in stocks would achieve a larger capital gain and a slightly higher yield in periods of rising prices but it would, of course, be subject to greater capital shrinkage in periods of falling prices.

Another consideration in establishing the initial proportion is the

level at which stock prices happen to be at the time. If it is thought
to be historically high, a smaller percentage should be committed
to stocks, and vice versa if it is thought to be historically low. In
this respect, the criticism would naturally be raised that careful
judgment is required—judgment not only of the relative highness or
lowness of current prices but also of the potential range of fluctuation over the next few years. But dependence on judgment is something that formula plans are supposedly designed to avoid. In answer, it can only be said that if *some* discrimination and *some*
common sense are used at the start, subsequent results should justify
their employment.

In this connection, it may be well to point out that two constant-
ratio plans starting out under reciprocally different proportions—for
instance, 60/40 and 40/60—will always wind up showing the same
capital gain, if we assume that stock prices have traversed a complete *round-trip cycle;* that is, have returned to their starting point.
A little reflection will make this clear. In the declining phase of the
market, the transfers from bonds to stocks will be a slightly greater
percentage of the total fund if the stock/bond ratio is 60/40 than
if it is 40/60; contrariwise, in a rising phase, the transfers from
stocks to bonds will be a slightly smaller percentage of the total
fund if the ratio is 60/40 than if it is 40/60. To put it another way,
and perhaps more simply, the dollar amounts of the transfers from
bonds to stocks and stocks to bonds will be the same for both types
at various action points.

In this respect, the author's position is different from that taken
by Cottle and Whitman (4), who say:

The identical "round-trip" capital gain for each plan results from the fact
that in a declining market the transfers from bonds to stock under a 35/65
or 65/35 plan (or any other pair of inverse ratios) will be the same
percentage of the market value of each fund. Likewise, in a rising market
the transfers from stocks to bonds will be equal percentages of the
market value of each fund.

The dollar amounts of the transfers prove to be equal but their
percentages of the market value of each fund are not equal, as above

stated. This point can be clarified through a simple arithmetical example. Let us assume that we start with two funds of the same dollar amount ($10,000) and apply a 60/40 stock/bond ratio to one and a 40/60 ratio to the other. The calculation would proceed along the following lines:

RISING MARKET

	TOTAL FUND	STOCKS	BONDS	TRANFER	
				Dollars	Per cent
60/40 FUND					
Initial position	$10,000	$6,000	$4,000		
Position after an assumed					
25% rise in stocks	11,500	7,500	4,000		
Revalue to 60/40 position	11,500	6,900	4,600	600	5.22
40/60 FUND					
Initial position	$10,000	$4,000	$6,000		
Position after an assumed					
25% rise in stocks	11,000	5,000	6,000		
Revalue to 40/60 position	11,000	4,400	6,600	600	5.46

DECLINING MARKET

	TOTAL FUND	STOCKS	BONDS	TRANFER	
				Dollars	Per cent
60/40 FUND					
Initial position	$10,000	$6,000	$4,000		
Position after an assumed					
25% decline in stocks	8,500	4,500	4,000		
Revalue to 60/40 position	8,500	5,100	3,400	600	7.06
40/60 FUND					
Initial position	$10,000	$4,000	$6,000		
Position after an assumed					
25% decline in stocks	9,000	3,000	6,000		
Revalue to 40/60 position	9,000	3,600	5,400	600	6.66

From the above, it is clearly seen that, while the dollar amounts of transfer are the same for both funds in any given percentage of rise or decline in the aggressive portion, the percentages of such transfer relative to the total fund are slightly greater for the 60/40 fund in a declining market and slightly greater for a 40/60 fund in a rising market.

Stock-bond transfers are maximized only under the 50/50 plan and, as a result, the 50/50 proportion yields the greatest amount of capital appreciation in any complete round-trip cycle. The value of the fund under a 50/50 plan will be greater at the end than under any other stock/bond ratio, assuming any one complete round trip. This is the reason why the 50/50 plan is generally preferred over any other combination ratio; also, it eases the problem of computation. But if stock prices were to take off on a generally rising trend and never return to the starting point, then the plan with the greatest part of the fund in stocks would show the best results. If stock prices were to go into a long decline, then the plan with the smallest part of the fund in stocks would show the best results.

CONSTANT-DOLLAR VERSUS CONSTANT-RATIO PLAN

As Tables 1 and 4 indicate, the constant-dollar plan will produce somewhat better results over one complete round-trip cycle than will the constant-ratio plan. The greater profit shown by the former is due to the fact that, at every transfer point as prices rise, the whole amount of the dollar gain is protected by transfer to the defensive portion. Thus, the defensive portion constitutes a larger part of the total fund when prices start to decline. Conversely, when prices start to rise, such as in Period 8 in Tables 1 and 4, a larger part of the total fund is in aggressive securities than under constant-ratio operation. Under the latter, only enough of the gain is transferred at each action point to restore the *ratio* of the two portions.

Of course the tables apply to a fairly regular, rhythmic fluctuation of the DJIA around a hypothetical level; they illustrate a round-trip price cycle. But from practical experience, we know that actual prices are not always so obliging that they follow a pattern of regular cyclical periodicity. The real world of stock prices is sometimes marked by violent ups and downs, sometimes by relative inactivity and absence of fluctuation, and sometimes by fairly long periods of rising or falling prices without the occurrence of any appreciable intermediate fluctuations or temporary price corrections.

In this real world of prices, the constant-ratio plan may be expected to perform somewhat better than the constant-dollar plan. Over a long period of years, during which prices are steadily rising, constant-ratio operation would produce more satisfactory results because a specified percentage of a *growing portfolio* is kept in aggressive securities, and this makes for better appreciation possibilities in the long run. Under constant-dollar operation, larger dollar sales of stocks are required at each transfer point on the way up, and thus the aggressive portion becomes a progressively smaller part of the total fund. Moreover, in any market decline over a long period, the constant-ratio plan will never run out of a defensive fund, which is always a predetermined percentage of the total. However, we have already seen that the defensive portion of a constant-dollar plan could well be exhausted if the price decline were precipitate enough; and the fund would then become immobilized if the decline continued. A constant-ratio plan would also be better able to withstand a long, uninterrupted price decline because smaller dollar purchases of stocks are required at each transfer point than under a constant-dollar plan. The relatively smaller amounts held in the aggressive portion provide better protection against the decline. The constant-ratio plan necessarily provides for less aggressive purchasing on a decline and for less aggressive selling on an advance than does the constant-dollar plan. The latter deals in absolute dollar sums while the former deals only in percentages, which helps to explain why the constant-ratio idea is in a more strategic position to take advantage of the capital-gain-producing opportunities presented by price movements of fairly long duration.

INSTITUTIONAL APPLICATIONS OF THE CONSTANT-RATIO PLAN

THE YALE UNIVERSITY PLAN

For the investment management of its endowment fund, Yale University decided, in 1939, to employ a constant-ratio formula plan. In view of the conditions affecting the security markets at that time, and in view of the prospective outlook, it was decided that no more than 30 per cent of the total fund would be initially committed to stocks. It was felt that such an aggressive position, while rather arbitrary, would satisfy the expectations of the fund managers by making possible a higher current yield as well as allowing for the possibility of some additional capital gain. Ordinary income would normally be withdrawn to help defray current operating costs of the university, while any capital gains would be retained in the fund for reinvestment.

For operational purposes, the constant-ratio plan was applied as follows:

Price Rise. From a starting position of 30 per cent, the aggressive portion would not be reduced until it had appreciated to 40 per cent of the fund. Approximately a 55 per cent increase in the value of the stock portion would be required to reach the action point, as shown in the following example, which assumes a starting fund of $100,000.

STOCK PORTION	BOND PORTION	TOTAL FUND	PERCENTAGE OF PORTFOLIO *Aggressive*	*Defensive*
$30,000	$70,000	$100,000	30	70
46,600	70,000	116,600	40	60

The $16,600 capital appreciation represents about a 55½ per cent gain, based upon the original stock portion of $30,000.

When the transfer point was reached, sufficient stocks would be sold to bring the stock portion down to 35 per cent of the total. Applying this to our example, enough stocks are sold to realize approximately $5800, which is added to the defensive portion. The fund is then divided as follows:

STOCK PORTION	BOND PORTION	TOTAL FUND	PERCENTAGE OF PORTFOLIO *Aggressive*	*Defensive*
$40,800	$75,800	$116,600	35	65

If the price rise continued and the aggressive portion again appreciated to 40 per cent of the total, another sale of stocks would again reduce the aggressive portion to 35 per cent.

Price Decline. If prices declined, the aggressive portion would not be increased until it had depreciated to 15 per cent of the total fund. When this point was reached, enough bonds would be sold and enough stocks bought to raise the stock portion to 20 per cent of the total. Should the decline continue, the process would be repeated each time the aggressive portion declined to 15 per cent of the total fund. With a starting fund of $100,000, the movements would be as follows:

STOCK PORTION	BOND PORTION	TOTAL FUND	PERCENTAGE OF PORTFOLIO *Aggressive*	*Defensive*
$30,000	$70,000	$100,000	30	70
12,500	70,000	82,500	15	85
16,500	66,000	82,500	20	80

Since World War II, Yale has seen fit to modify both the transfer point and the stock/bond ratio, no doubt because higher yields have been needed to meet steadily rising costs. The first revision called for reduction in the aggressive portion when it had appreciated to 45 rather than 40 per cent of the fund. This change was made in 1950. In the following year, it was decided that, when the 45 per cent figure was reached, the aggressive-portion reduction would be to 37½ rather than 35 per cent. So far as the procedure for adding to stocks in a price decline is concerned, the present Yale policy is not to be bound by any prefixed transfer point; stocks need not decline to 15 per cent of the total before action is taken to raise the percentage. (17) In fact, the most recent Yale policy, which reflects the current situation, indicates that the university has deviated even more from any sort of strict compliance with the requirements of a constant-ratio plan. No longer are transfer points based on changes in stock/bond ratios. Rather, increasing emphasis is now placed on individual stock selection. What remains of formula operation is devoted to an attempt to establish attractive purchase levels for individual stocks, rather than for the market as a whole.

THE KENYON COLLEGE PLAN

Kenyon College adopted a modified form of a constant-ratio principle in the early part of 1941. (2, 6, 17, 18, 19) Prior to that time, an investment committe had sole responsibility for the management of the portfolio. The committee faced two principal problems: (1) the problem of security selection, and (2) the problem of proper timing of purchases and sales. A rule that required unanimous committee agreement increased the difficulty of reaching immediate decisions. To relieve the committee of the responsibility for proper timing, a formula-plan principle was introduced. This facilitated committee action, because the only remaining major problem was security selection. In implementing the formula principle, it was decided that a normal ratio for the aggressive portion to bear to the total fund was 40 per cent. The only limiting feature was a requirement that no stocks would be purchased when the aggressive portion of the fund was greater than 40 per cent and no stocks should be sold whenever the portion was less than 40 per cent. The exact points of transfer from stocks to bonds (above 40 per cent) and from bonds to stocks (below 40 per cent) were left to the discretion of the committee. It was felt that this would permit greater flexibility of operation and would also make the total fund more responsive to current developments that affected security prices.

The committee has a schedule that requires only three meetings a year and permits special meetings in the event of any emergency. Whenever the committee meets, it reviews the portfolio and determines the proportionate changes in its stock and bond portions. If, in the light of current conditions, the committee considers the stock portion sufficiently above 40 per cent to require adjustment, it sells stocks to an extent that reduces the stock/bond ratio to 40/60. If the stock portion is below 40 per cent, the committee may purchase sufficient stocks to raise the ratio to 40/60. But the committee does not feel constrained to wait for a certain minimum amount of fluctuation before acting. On one occasion, the stock portion was allowed to increase to 48 per cent before stocks were sold; on other occasions, transfers were made when variations from the normal ratio were as slight as 2 or 3 per cent.

The committee has been particularly gratified by the results, since 1942, of its plan. After the plan's adoption, the committee bought stocks at such market low points as those of the spring of 1942, the fall of 1946, and the summer of 1949. On the selling side, it selected the middle of 1943, early 1946, late 1948, and the early months of 1951 and 1953.[1] How much of this commendable timing can be attributed to the formula plan and how much to the exceptionally good judgment of the committee is something that cannot be determined.

[1] The reader is referred to the Frontispiece and Figure 2 for information about movement of stock prices. The upper part of the Frontispiece contains a curve made up of vertical lines, each line representing the range of 50 industrials during the corresponding month; for the same period, 1935 through 1956, the average (not in terms of monthly range) is given for 20 utilities and also the average for 20 railroads. Figure 2, which shows only the fluctuations in the DJIA, affords a better perspective, perhaps, of the relative price relationships between 1942 and 1953.

Chapter 4

The Nature of Variable- Ratio Plans

The operation of a variable-ratio plan can best be understood by comparing its principal features with those of the equalization plan. Under the constant-ratio variation of the latter, an attempt is made to maintain the *same* percentage of the fund in aggressive securities at all levels of the market. Whether the market is high or low, the predetermined stock/bond relationship is maintained, regardless of changes in stock price levels. Thus, if it is a 50/50 plan, 50 per cent of the fund is aggressive when the market may be at peak levels, and conversely only 50 per cent of the fund is aggressive when the market may be at very depressed levels. The constant-ratio plan is, therefore, open to the criticism that it fails to take the fullest advantage of changing price levels. To this objection, the variable-ratio plan provides an answer.

OPERATION OF THE PLAN

In variable-ratio operation, progressively lower percentages of the total fund are kept in the aggressive portion as prices rise and progressively higher percentages as prices fall. In other words, an attempt is made to vary or change the aggressive portion in accordance with price changes, and not in disregard of them. But if

47

a buying-and-selling schedule is to be predetermined, the plan necessarily involves more long-range forecasting than does either the constant-ratio or the constant-dollar plan.

The fund manager who is to be guided in his timing operations by a variable-ratio plan must first of all answer these fundamental questions:

1. What is a normal or average level of stock prices at which a 50/50 stock/bond relationship will be established?
2. What will constitute a high level of stock prices?
3. What will constitute a low level of stock prices?

In other words, he must decide in advance what he estimates will be the average or normal future trend around which he expects stock prices to fluctuate. Then he must try to define, somehow, the extent or degree of the expected fluctuations above and below this norm, that is, anticipate the upper and lower limits between which future stock prices will move. The answers to these three questions are crucial because the entire success or failure of a variable-ratio plan depends upon them.

A fourth problem—of somewhat less magnitude than the first three—is the choice of an index to be used as a measure of the fluctuations in the stock-price levels upon which transfer points are based. Most variable-ratio plans rely upon one or another published index, the one most frequently used being the DJIA, which for all practical purposes has been found most satisfactory. Its record is consistent and historically long, providing a continuous series of published data dating from 1897 to the present; its computation is mathematically accurate; its figures are published daily; and it is perhaps the best-known and most universally acceptable index that is designed to reflect general market conditions. Since March 4, 1957, Standard & Poor's Corporation has published a new index, Standard & Poor's Daily Price Index (which can be called the "Standard 500" to distinguish it from its predecessors).[1] This new index

---

[1] Prior to March 4, 1957, Standard & Poor's Corporation was publishing two completely separate stock indexes, one daily, the other weekly. The daily

may prove to correspond more closely than has the DJIA to the monthly average of all listed stocks published by the New York Stock Exchange. Therefore it may eventually displace the DJIA for use in formula-plan calculations.

Table 5 illustrates the mechanics of operation of a typical variable-ratio plan. Here a sample buying-and-selling schedule is set

TABLE 5. VARIABLE-RATIO PLAN

(Sample schedule of buying and selling points and percentage distribution of funds)

| DJIA | PERCENTAGE OF PORTFOLIO | |
	Defensive	Aggressive
560 and above	90	10
520–559	80	20
480–519	70	30
440–479	60	40
400–439	50	50
360–399	40	60
320–359	30	70
280–319	20	80
280 and below	10	90

up with the DJIA as our index and with the assumption that transfers from stocks to bonds, or vice versa, will be made with each 40-

---

index was based on 90 stocks, comprising 50 industrials, 20 railroads, and 20 utilities. For this index the base was 1926. The weekly index was more accurate, being based upon 480 stocks, including 420 industrials, 20 railroads, and 40 utilities (the base period was 1935 to 1939). However, it was not widely distributed, and the fact that it was published only once a week weighed against it.

The "Standard 500," designed to overcome these difficulties, is based upon 500 stocks, comprising 425 industrials, 25 railroads, and 50 utilities; the market value of these 500 stocks is equal to more than 90 per cent of the market value of all stocks traded on the New York Stock Exchange. Ten, instead of the conventional 100, serves as the base, in terms of which index numbers are given. The years, 1941 through 1943, were adopted as the base period, the values for this period being equated to ten.

The "Standard 500," like the DJIA, is available both on an hourly and a daily basis. A compilation of the same figures classified by industries is published weekly. These, together, supplant all the old Standard & Poor's indexes.

From a statistical standpoint the "Standard 500" is probably the most accurate index available. Distortions that might result from stock dividends, stock splits, issuance of subscription rights, etc., are avoided by the use of a system of weights in which the price of each stock is multiplied by the number of shares outstanding.

point change in the Average. Opposite each 40-point trading range
is what might be considered an appropriate distribution of the
fund between the aggressive and defensive portions. Our assumed normal area is the 400–439 range. If we were initiating a
variable-ratio plan under the assumed conditions, and if the DJIA
happened to be in the 400–439 range at the time, one-half of the
fund would be committed to stocks and one-half to bonds or other
defensive securities. If the Average subsequently moved into the
440–479 range, enough stocks would be sold to reduce the aggressive portion to 40 per cent of the total. The proceeds, of course,
would be reinvested in bonds. At each transfer point, the fund
would be revalued, the total market values of the defensive and aggressive portions calculated, and the two totaled. The percentages
applicable to the new trading range would then be applied to the
total fund, and the results would be the dollar amounts that should
be committed to the two portions after the transfer had been
effected.

For example, let us suppose that we start with a fund of
$100,000 and that the DJIA at the time is in the 400–439 range.
Consequently, we establish our fund with $50,000 in stocks and
$50,000 in bonds. Now assume that DJIA moves up to the 440–479
range. Suppose, then, that our revaluation is as follows:

STOCK PORTION	BOND PORTION	TOTAL FUND	PERCENTAGE OF PORTFOLIO Aggressive	Defensive
$64,000	$51,000	$115,000		
46,000	69,000	115,000	40	60

The required action is the sale of stocks worth $18,000 and the in-
vestment of the $18,000 in bonds. These figures merely illustrate
the principle, but our basic assumption that, as the Average moved
up 40 points, our stock fund would appreciate to $64,000 and our
bond fund to $51,000 is perhaps not too unrealistic.

The principles illustrated above apply to all other transfer
areas. As our index moves above normal, the aggressive portion is
steadily reduced. When the Average gets to 560 and above, it is as-

sumed to be at an historical high. At that time, it should be noticed, only a *minimum percentage*—10 per cent—remains aggressive.

If, having initiated our plan, our index moves below normal, we steadily increase the aggressive portion until the Average gets to 280 or below, which is assumed to be a historically low area, when a *maximum percentage* is aggressive.

It should be noted that transfer is rarely carried to the point that the stock/bond ratio is 100/0 in a declining market, or 0/100 in a rising market. The plans that do provide for this sort of action are the exception. Most variable-ratio plans provide for a minimum percentage that will remain aggressive on the upside and a maximum aggressive percentage on the downside. Once the market index moves out of the trading range—that is, either above the range in which the minimum aggressive percentage is attained or below that in which the maximum percentage is attained—the fund becomes temporarily immobilized. But no matter how high the DJIA goes, some proportion of stocks—if only a minimum—is retained, and the fund thus participates to a limited extent in the benefits of rising prices. And no matter how low the Average goes, some reserve fund is always available to give some element of stability, both in price and income, to the total fund.

The operation of a variable-ratio plan is illustrated in Table 6, which is constructed with the hypothetical conditions and assumptions of Tables 1 and 4 to permit a comparison of the various formula plans. The shifts in the portfolio managed with a variable-ratio plan show that this method produces better results from a capital-gain standpoint than do either of the equalization plans. The difference can be attributed to the fact that the variable-ratio method is specifically designed to take maximum advantage of changing price levels. It requires more dollar sales of stocks on the way up and more dollar purchases on the way down. For this reason, it is theoretically in the best protective position against a price decline when market levels are high and it is also in the best protective position to capitalize on a price rise when market levels are low. The variable-ratio idea introduces an element of flexibility not available in equalization-plan operation.

DETERMINATION OF THE STOCK-PRICE TREND

In establishing any variable-ratio plan, a crucial problem is the determination of the future trend of stock prices that is realistic and can be expected to divide, more or less equally, future market fluctuations. A trend line that is unrealistically high will lead to a maximum build-up of the aggressive portion too quickly; as prices decline, the fund might well become immobilized before the lower limit of the trading zone is reached. A trend line that is too low will lead to the disposal of stocks too early in a price rise; the minimum aggressive percentage might be reached well before the top of the rise, and many profitable opportunities will thus be sacrificed. Poor trend determination could also lead to long periods of complete inactivity. Such a situation would occur during rather violent market fluctuations and during periods when the secular trend might be changing to produce a permanent departure of prices from the intermediate trend.

The determination of a proper trend line, then, is important because it is the very basis for establishing the variable-ratio proportions between the aggressive and defensive funds. If, at the outset, a variable-ratio plan is based on a poorly constructed trend line, its results in all likelihood will prove correspondingly disappointing. Fortunately, we are not entirely without help in finding a solution to this problem; certain statistical tools are available. A fairly satisfactory price trend can be defined by the moving-average method, by the projected-trend method, or by the intrinsic-value method. These three methods are discussed in detail in the following sections.

TABLE 6. VARIABLE-RATIO PLAN

(A hypothetical example based on a $50,000 portfolio and accompanying sample schedule)

PERIOD	CHANGES IN PORTFOLIO	DEFENSIVE PORTION	AGGRESSIVE PORTION	TOTAL VALUE OF PORTFOLIO
1	DJIA at 400 (starting point)	$25,000	$25,000	$50,000
2	DJIA advances to 440	25,000	27,500	52,500
	Sell aggressive and buy defensive securities to reduce the former to 40% of the fund	31,500	21,000	52,500
3	DJIA advances to 484	31,500	23,100	54,600
	Sell aggressive and buy defensive securities to reduce the former to 30% of the fund	38,220	16,380	54,600
4	DJIA advances to 532	38,220	18,018	56,238
	Sell aggressive and buy defensive securities to reduce the former to 20% of the fund	44,990	11,248	56,238
5	DJIA declines to 480	44,990	10,123	55,113
	Sell defensive and buy aggressive securities to increase the latter to 30% of the fund	38,579	16,534	55,113
6	DJIA declines to 432	38,579	14,881	53,460
	Sell defensive and buy aggressive securities to increase the latter to 50% of the fund	26,730	26,730	53,460
7	DJIA declines to 388	26,730	24,057	50,787
	Sell defensive and buy aggressive securities to increase the latter to 60% of the fund	20,315	30,472	50,787
8	DJIA declines to 350	20,315	27,425	47,740
	Sell defensive and buy aggressive securities to increase the latter to 70% of the fund	14,322	33,418	47,740
9	DJIA advances to 385	14,322	36,760	51,082
	Sell aggressive and buy defensive securities to reduce the former to 60% of the fund	20,433	30,649	51,082
10	DJIA advances to 424	20,433	33,714	54,147
	Sell aggressive and buy defensive securities to reduce the former to 50% of the fund	27,073	27,074	54,147
11	DJIA declines 5.6% to 400	27,073	25,558	52,631

MOVING-AVERAGE METHOD

The construction and maintenance of a moving average are fairly simple statistical operations: An average figure is continually applied to a series of "running" or constantly changing basic data for a specified time period.

If we are calculating an arithmetic average, we add up the figures and divide the total by the number of figures added. The same principle is used to construct a moving average, except that the process is carried one step further to keep it continuously applicable to a changing situation. For example, suppose that we want to construct a moving average of a stock's price for a period of 5 years, say, 1946 through 1950. A representative figure might be the average of the high and low prices at which the stock sold during the year. These five hypothetical average figures are arranged in a row opposite their respective years. They are totaled and the sum is then divided by 5 to get an average 5-year figure, viz:

YEAR	AVERAGE PRICE	MOVING AVERAGE FOR PERIOD
1946	60	
1947	55	
1948	50	
1949	45	
1950	55	53 1946–50
1951	70	55 1947–51

The average for the 1946–1950 period is 53. But when the data for another year become available, we wish to move this average forward, so that we have an average for the 1947–1951 period. To do this, we drop from our total the figure for the earliest year, 1946, and add to the total the figure for the latest year, 1951. The new total is also divided by 5, and the resulting figure, 55, is the average for the 1947–1951 period. This process is repeated each time that new data for the series become available. The result is a moving-average line, which, when charted with the basic data, produces a trend line that smooths out the fluctuations of the underlying figures, indicates the direction in which the average figure is moving, and provides a level around which the basic data should tend to fluctuate.

If a decision is made to use a moving average as a means of arriving at a trend, a major problem is this: What time period should the average represent? Should the moving average be based on a short period, say, 3 or 4 years, or would a longer period of 20 to 25 years be preferable? The selection of a proper time period for the average is quite important, for a trend line, to be useful, must be neither too sensitive nor too insensitive. Too short a period would result in too much fluctuation of the average and would make the trend line correspond too closely with the movements of the basic data. In that case, needless overtrading—caused by short-term fluctuations—might result. A well-constructed moving average should eliminate the effects of short-term fluctuations and principally reflect the longer-run swings of prices. On the other hand, too long a time period might result in an unrealistic trend line—one that might fail to equally divide the extreme high and low areas of future fluctuations and so permit the aggressive fund to be sold out too soon in a rising market or to become fully invested too soon in a falling market.

There has been considerable experimentation with time periods in an attempt to discover one that will meet the indicated requirements. Vassar College originally used a 5-year period but later adopted a 10-year period as the basis for a moving average of the DJIA mean annual high and low prices. Similarly, Francis I. duPont & Co. has set up its Institutional Plan, on the basis of a 10-year moving average of the monthly mean prices of the DJIA from 1895 to the present. This, in effect, amounts to a 120-month average.

A recent study of moving averages investigated the relative merits of 6-, 10-, and 15-year periods. The basis for the study was the data of the years 1926 through 1950, the averages being constructed from the mean annual high and low prices of the DJIA. (4) The results showed that the 15-year moving average produced the greatest capital appreciation and the 6-year average the least. The latter proved to be out of step with the basic data for most of the period—a shortcoming that would have resulted in some untimely purchases and sales—and it also exhibited too great a degree of cyclical movement of its own to make it useful as a trend line. But although the 15-year average proved the best for the particular period of study, it must be remembered that the amplitude of fluctuation in the basic data was of sufficient magnitude to favor the longer time period; that is, it just happened that the 15-year average worked best for the 1926–1950 period. Whether the future will see fluctuations of a similar degree and periodicity is a matter that is not subject to prophecy. If it does, then the 15-year average may continue to prove workable. If it does not, then a different time period would be worthy of consideration.

Another problem in the construction of a moving average is this: Should some adjustment be made for the factor of long-term growth? Past observation of stock prices, as represented by the DJIA, has shown that there is unmistakable evidence of a slow, long-term upward trend that has averaged to about 3 per cent a year. If a simple moving average without adjustment is used, each year's figure is given as much weight in the final average as is that of any other year. To overcome this difficulty and to make due allowance for the growth factor, it has been suggested that the moving average be adjusted for the growth that has presumably taken place during the time period on which the average is based. (17) If we assume that a 3 per cent per year growth will continue in the future—as it has, approximately, in the past—and if we also assume the use of a 15-year moving average, then the figure for the fifteenth year would be about 45 per cent above that for the first year if no cyclical fluctuation at all had taken place. Averaged out over the whole 15-year period, an adjustment of 22½ per cent would be called for; it could be accomplished by adding this percentage each year to the 15-year average. If the assumed growth rate is maintained, a moving average adjusted in this manner is likely to produce results somewhat superior to those of an unadjusted index.[2]

---

[2] However, this assumes that the secular trend will always continue upward at the same rate. If it changes suddenly—either levels off or declines—the unadjusted index would probably prove superior to the adjusted.

In summary, then, the moving-average method cannot be said to be without merit as a means of constructing a realistic trend line.[3] In its favor, it may be said that it is peculiarly able to adapt itself to changing conditions and also provide the flexibility necessary in dealing with dynamic situations. In addition, it is so constructed that its movements are predicated upon movements in the underlying data, and it is therefore unlikely to develop any protracted divergence from the real figures. However, as has been indicated, a very great deal in the successful application of this device to formula-plan operations depends upon the selection of the proper time period and the decision on adjustment for annual growth. Furthermore, the cyclical fluctuations in stock prices in the past have certainly not displayed the regularity of amplitude or periodicity of movement that would make a moving average most advantageous; nor is such regularity likely to be a characteristic of the future. In view of these mechanical limitations, the moving-average method must be handled with a certain amount of caution and skepticism.

PROJECTED-TREND METHOD

The second method of establishing a trend of stock prices is to project a line that has been determined either by careful observation of past stock price movements or by involved statistical procedures. It is doubtful, however, that mathematical precision is of sufficient usefulness to warrant the considerable amount of effort and professional talent necessary to secure it. A carefully constructed graph with a trend line manually fitted to past data is commonly relied on in determining the trend that is to be projected into the future.

Like the moving-average method, the projected-trend method is entirely dependent upon market history. When the fluctuations of the DJIA between 1897 and the present are plotted on a semilogarithmic or ratio scale, a long upward trend is evident. When

---

[3] Some problems connected with the use of the moving average for long-range trend determination will be dealt with more fully in Chapter 8.

one straight line is drawn to connect the extreme lows and a second is drawn to connect the extreme highs, a range, or channel, of movement is apparent. (The upper line is drawn under the high of 1929 and the lower line above the low of 1932 because a trend, by its very nature, is invalid if it takes account of *abnormal* periods of fluctuation.)

The lines that trace the upper and lower limits of normal fluctuation are remarkably parallel; if a line is drawn halfway between them, a reasonably accurate average is obtained. By reading off approximate values of the DJIA that correspond to the middle line, a price level at which a 50/50 stock/bond ratio should be established can be located. Given this point, it is possible to set up a buying-and-selling schedule that provides for successive reductions in the aggressive portion to a minimum position when the top line is reached and for successive additions to the aggressive portion to a maximum position when the bottom line is reached.[4]

When the projected-trend method is used, it is crucial that the projection be made as accurately as possible, since this projection is to be the basis of decisions to buy and sell in the future. The trend is usually shown on a graph in one of two ways, which differ only in the scale divisions used. In both cases the horizontal axis conventionally shows time (in days, weeks, months, or years, according to choice), and the vertical axis stock prices in dollars.

In the case of the arithmetic graph, the vertical axis is divided into equal segments, the type of scale so familiar to newspaper readers. The trend shown on such a graph is called an arithmetic trend. When a stock price changes by the same number of dollars per year, say 10 points, the arithmetic trend will appear as a straight line.

The geometric trend, on the other hand, which is a trend graphed on semilogarithmic paper, shows percentage or rate of change. When the dollar stock value is graphed on the log axis, the resulting geometric trend line represents changes in stock prices

[4] The method described is the well-known Keystone Seven-Step Plan, shown in Figure 3 and discussed in Chapter 5.

not in absolute units but in *percentages*. The geometric trend will therefore be a straight line not when the stock increases by the same number of points each year but rather by a constant percentage, say 10 per cent a year.

Which trend line is to be preferred for the variable-ratio plan? It is impossible to give an unqualified answer, since the past record of stock prices as represented by the DJIA is a combination of all kinds of fluctuations—many rates of rise and decline. Price movements in the past have not been obliging enough to give straight lines when measured either by absolute or percentage changes of price. However, since 1947, the yearly advance of the DJIA has represented more nearly a constant-percentage than a constant-dollar increase, indicating that a stronger argument can probably be made for use of the geometric-trend graph in the immediate future.

A minor problem in connection with the projected-trend method is the period of years to which the trend is to be fitted. In this case, the answer can be somewhat more definite: The period should be the longest for which reliable figures are available. The longer the period, the greater is the likelihood that different past rates of growth will tend to offset and compensate each other. It is for this reason that the DJIA is a preferable source of data, for it supplies a single, continuous series from 1897 to the present. The only qualification is the one, mentioned earlier, that abnormal fluctuations should be disregarded in fitting the trend line. Of course, if the secular trend of prices ever changes rather sharply in the future, the investor will face the annoying problem of trying to decide whether a certain price movement is an abnormal cyclical fluctuation or whether it is a type of movement more or less in line with the degree of change in the trend.

There is a final problem in connection with the use of the projected-trend method for determining the trend line: What should be done if future fluctuations of stock prices develop a pattern that shows more or less permanent departure from the projected trend? Today, any plot of stock-price trend, whether arithmetic or geo-

metric would have an upward tendency. (This would necessarily
be so because the basic data exhibit steady, long-term upward
growth.) Therefore, any projection of the trend would constitute an
assumption of continued growth. But suppose this assumption
proves unwarranted. Suppose that, in the future, stock prices level
off over the longer term, or even go into a mild secular downtrend.
Actual prices would then have departed from the trend, which
would cease to function effectively. While the chance that this sort
of thing will happen in the near future is probably not very great,
a critical evaluation of the projected-trend method must take it
into account. The answer, should the problem arise, is to so change
the trend projection that it conforms more closely with the changed
basic conditions. But this is not really as simple as its sounds. A
great deal of judgment must enter into such a decision, and two
factors are of vital importance: (1) *when* to alter or refit the trend,
and (2) *how much* alteration is necessary. To reproject the trend
too soon might be to jump to conclusions—what appeared to be
the beginning of a new set of conditions might turn out to be
merely an abnormal development in the old pattern. On the other
hand, to wait too long to reproject the trend—to wait, that is, until
a new set of conditions was readily observable—would result in
many ill-timed commitments and a serious distortion of the buying-
and-selling schedule (based, as it would be, on an unrealistic, mal-
functioning trend).[5] The projected-trend line is very inflexible in
this respect; unlike the moving average, it does not readily adapt
itself to changing conditions. But while a precise and definite
answer to this problem cannot be given, it may be sufficient for
present purposes to be aware that the difficulty might exist at some
future time and that the investor should make due mental allowance for it. For, in the final analysis, it is the individual investor
who must choose and decide; the trend projection he selects must
be the one that appears to him to be most satisfactory and reasonable—in the light of current knowledge—as a description of the general course of future stock prices.

[5] This problem will be discussed more fully in Chapter 8.

INTRINSIC-VALUE METHOD

Unlike the moving-average and projected-trend methods, the intrinsic-value method does not rely on market history to arrive at a trend line. Rather, it seeks to define a "normal" price level by means of an analysis of factors that can be considered determinants of security values. Some of these factors are earnings per share, dividends, book values, yields, price-earnings ratios, and ratios of stock prices to dividends. The basic assumption, of course, is that a sufficiently constant relationship exists between stock prices and these various measures of "intrinsic value" to provide a satisfactory normal price level.

"Intrinsic value," however, is a rather nebulous concept. Does the term imply a long-run normal value for a security or a shorter-term value based upon the foreseeable and probable movement of some independent variable, such as earning power? If the basic factors that are employed as determinants of intrinsic value are constantly changing, then intrinsic value itself must be constantly changing. The further into the future that such a concept of value is projected, the more dangerous become the consequences of relying too heavily upon its validity. On this subject, Plum and Humphrey say:

> There are few clues to the long-term future, which is the most speculative factor involved in buying common stocks at all. Security analysis may help in choosing the more attractive investment opportunities, but even this may involve speculative assumptions as to the far-distant future. A more reliable forecast is the probable trend of earnings in the immediate future and business forecasting of the better variety may possibly be of some help in this respect. (14)

If the intrinsic-value trend line is to have maximum validity, its construction must be based upon an analysis of factors that are relatively current in nature and that can be projected into the near-term future with reasonable assurance of accuracy or, at least, a minimum departure from what will turn out to be the actual result. What factors should be considered, then, in appraising intrinsic value for the short term? Graham and Dodd (8) list the following, presumably in order of relative importance:

  a. Earnings
  b. Dividends
  c. Assets
  d. Capital Structure
  e. Terms of the issue
  f. Others

They list additional items under the heading of future-value factors:

  a. Management and reputation
  b. Competitive conditions and prospects
  c. Possible and probable changes in volume, price, and costs.

The authors go on to say:

In the usual case the most important single factor determining value is now held to be the indicated average future earning power. Intrinsic value would then be found by first estimating this earning power and then multiplying that estimate by an appropriate "capitalization factor." (8)

Security analysts who lean toward the intrinsic-value method stress the importance of differentiating between value and price. The usual method of determining intrinsic value is subdivided into successive stages roughly as follows:

  1. Estimate near-future earnings of a stock.
  2. Estimate near-future dividends.
  3. Combine the earnings and dividend estimates into a single, adjusted figure.
  4. Calculate an average price-earnings ratio that is likely to prevail in the near future.
  5. Multiply the adjusted earnings figure (3) by the average price-earnings ratio to obtain an intrinsic value.

The final step in the analysis is to compare the calculated intrinsic value with the actual current market price to determine evidence of over- or undervaluation. If the market price is only slightly greater than the intrinsic value, the stock would not be purchased in any event; if the market price is greater by approximately 10 per cent and if some shares are already owned, the shares would probably be sold, or at least a desirable selling level would be established. If the market price is below intrinsic value by approximately 20 per cent, stock would probably be purchased, or at least a desirable purchase level would be established.

In attempting to apply these principles to a formula plan, another complication is introduced. The trend line of a variable-ratio formula is generally based upon some recognized stock index or average, such as the DJIA. The problem, then, is to determine intrinsic value for such an average. Most of the principles of analysis that are cited above apply to individual stocks. But this does not mean that the principles are invalid for determining intrinsic value of a stock index. Either of two general methods may be used:

1. Determine intrinsic value for each individual stock in the index or average and then calculate a weighted average of the total of the separate values.

2. Determine intrinsic value for index as a whole by using aggregate data. In the case of the DJIA, the analyst is periodically supplied with such aggregate data as composite earnings and dividends. An average price-earnings ratio applied to an adjusted estimated-earnings figure would yield a calculated value that would represent an annual intrinsic value. From this figure, then, appropriate buying and selling schedules could be established.

Variable-ratio formula plans that employ an intrinsic-value trend line seem to give varying weight to the basic value determinants. Some give more weight to book values; others accord major importance to earnings; still others, to dividends. As far as earnings and dividend factors go, a recent study conducted on this subject revealed that

. . . although the *cyclical fluctuations* of stock prices and earnings appear to be more closely related than those for prices and dividends, the

reverse is true of the *long-term growth* of prices. The authors' studies
show clearly that the rate of secular growth of stock prices coincides
closely with that of the long-term rate of increase in dividends. (4)

In actual practice, several approaches have been tried in developing intrinsic values for use in the management of specific institutional funds. The First National Bank of Birmingham, Alabama,
after considerable statistical research, devised a method that uses,
as a trend, the average of the *adjusted book value* of each of the
30 stocks in the DJIA. Over the past 10 years, the bank has used
its variable-ratio plan for the investment supervision of its various
trusts and has been particularly gratified with the results. Another
intrinsic-value approach was devised by Benjamin Graham, who
calls it his Central-value method.[6] Graham's theory is to determine
a central value by computing the average earnings of the DJIA
for a 10-year period and then capitalizing this figure at twice the
current yield on high-grade bonds represented by Moody's Aaa
Corporate Bond Yield Average. Graham thus prefers to give the *earnings factor* greater weight in the determination of a trend line.
Still another intrinsic-value approach has recently been offered by
Edgar S. Genstein. (7) This plan emphasizes the *dividend factor* by
multiplying the current rate of dividends of the DJIA by a figure
that is supposed to represent a normal ratio of prices to dividends.

Evaluation. Obviously in favor of the intrinsic-value method
is the fact that the trend line would always be realistic and would
be unlikely to depart permanently from the basic data of market
prices. This is so because the same factors operate on the trend as
on the actual market price, with the exception of speculative factors
and those of a technical market nature. The latter are not allowed
to influence calculation of the trend; they can cause sharp price
fluctuations but they have no effect on the intrinsic value. There is
a real core of truth and common sense in an intrinsic-value trend
line, since it sets up a level around which actual market prices will
tend to fluctuate. Moreover, it is not tied to the past as rigidly as
are the moving-average and projected-trend methods, and so it

---

[6] The details and mechanics of the Birmingham and Graham plans are
more fully described in Chapter 5.

allows for that essential element of flexibility in meeting changing conditions in an uncertain future.

Since the method appears to rest largely on sound, basic economic relationships, its general principles are subject to little argument, but its actual mechanics of calculation may raise some minor doubts. For example, how do we know the proper capitalization rate for earnings or dividends? A minor change in the capitalization rate can easily make a big change in the ultimate result. How do we know that a rate of twice the current yield on high-grade bonds is the best rate? Why not three times or four times? Empirical observation of the past may have suggested a rate twice the bond yield, but who knows whether the relationship will continue to be desirable in the future? Also, what is the proper period for computing average earnings? Should it be 10 years, or should more weight be given to recent earnings? What, also, is the proper bond index to use to obtain a current yield? Slight variations in current yield, when multiplied to get a capitalization rate, may produce significant differences in the intrinsic value. And, in general, the required computation and calculation may be beyond the capability of the average investor, as may also be the appreciation and appraisal of fundamental economic and financial relationships that are so closely interwoven with the successful operation of the method.

The arguments against the intrinsic-value method are not without validity and, unfortunately, no real, precise answer to them is readily available. It is possible to say, though, that the method does perhaps represent a step forward in trend-line determination over either the moving-average or projected-trend methods. With all its minor mechanical imperfections, it probably represents the most reliable approach toward an accurate future price trend, which is really the core of all variable-ratio plans. Perhaps the accumulation of more experience as well as a readiness to change the mechanics of trend-line construction to ensure better adaptation to varying economic conditions might serve, in the long run, to remove many of the bases for criticism and so make the method ultimately the most productive of desirable results.

SUPPLEMENTARY CONSIDERATIONS

TRADING ZONES AND TRANSFER POINTS

After a trend line is determined by one or the other of the methods discussed above, it remains but to implement the variable-ratio plan by selecting zones above and below the line at which transfers will take place. This, too, involves considerable discrimination, for the zones should not be so narrow that they cause needless overtrading nor so broad that they result in lengthy periods of inactivity. The solution to the problem of zone selection depends largely on the nature and needs of the individual concerned and on his relative conservatism or aggressiveness.

Of course, the further apart the zones are, the greater will be the ultimate profit. Naturally, it would be desirable to achieve some measure of balance between the attempt to maximize profits and the reluctance to miss any important intermediate fluctuation. For all practical purposes, it would probably be satisfactory to separate zones at 10 or 15 per cent intervals, since, with such a schedule, an important fluctuation in either direction is not likely to be missed. Granting the basic presumption that stock prices will continue to fluctuate, one zone, or more, is almost certain to be crossed by each successive price movement. If the fluctuation is wide, many zones will be penetrated; if narrow, perhaps no more than one or two. Given a certain amount of fluctuation, the wider apart the zones are, the more will be gained. On the upside, stocks will be sold at higher prices, and on the downside, they will be bought at lower prices than if a narrower zone arrangement were used. Separation of zones on the basis of an absolute-number-of-points fluctuation would not, it is felt, be as satisfactory as separation by percentages. When the market is at a relatively low level, spacing zones by a specified number of points would require fairly large *percentage* movements in the index for zones to be crossed, and this might result in considerable periods of inactivity. On the other hand, when the market is at a relatively high level, small percentage movements in the index would cause frequent zone penetrations and thus call for a degree of overtrading, which might not conform to the best interests of the investor.

The distance between the upper and lower limits of the buying-and-selling schedule is also a matter for careful judgment. (38) The Keystone Seven-Step Plan provides for an upper level approximately 100 per cent above the lower level and this broad channel has been found fairly effective. If, however, either the upper or the lower limit is temporarily exceeded, the variable-ratio plan becomes, in effect, a constant-ratio plan with either a minimum percentage in stocks and a maximum in bonds, or vice versa. The width of the channel is expected to contain the limits (peaks and troughs) of future cyclical price fluctuations. The wider the channel, the more flexible will be the operation, for there is less likelihood that the formula plan will be "frozen" into a constant-ratio plan by a price movement beyond either limit. A good deal of success in this direction depends upon the extent to which the secular trend for the future is correctly forecast. This matter will be appraised more carefully in Chapter 8.

HALFWAY RULE AND DELAYING TACTICS

To achieve the greatest possible capital gain and to prevent overtrading in the aggressive portion whenever zones are crossed, certain defensive measures or, more properly, delaying tactics, have been developed. A very common method is the use of what is known as the *halfway rule*. This rule provides that no sale of aggressive securities is made below the trend line and no purchase of aggressive securities is made above the line. If a bull market should level out and be succeeded by a bear market of several years' duration, the halfway rule would keep an account from buying stocks too early in the decline, and conversely, from selling stocks too early in a subsequent rise. Also it would tend to ensure that the average cost of stocks accumulated in a decline would be lower, and the average selling price in a rise would be higher, than if such a rule were not observed. Thus a greater amount of capital gain would be preserved. In imposing this rule, however, the investor must content himself with long-term capital growth and with the benefits his formula plan can accrue to him by taking advantage of cyclical changes of trend. If, in the process, some possibly profitable transactions may have been missed by the failure to catch an intermediate fluctuation, or a so-called secondary reaction in a bull or bear market, he should not become impatient and disregard the rule. In the long run, more will be gained by observing the rule than by discarding it entirely or by arbitrarily disregarding its operation. The fact that most of the variable-ratio plans adapted to current institutional use today employ some variation of the halfway rule testifies to its successful operation. Additional comment on this point will be found in Chapter 5, where some of the practical applications of variable-ratio plans are discussed.

The halfway rule, while important, is only one of a number of tactics that call for delayed action; and all of these defensive measures have the effect of postponing full and complete action whenever a transfer zone is crossed. For instance, it may be considered prudent to sell or buy only a specified percentage (say, 25 or 30) of the required amount whenever an action point is reached, and to spread the balance out over a few months. To illustrate, suppose the price movement reaches a transfer point that calls for a reduction of 10 per cent in the aggressive portion. Let us say also that the indicated reduction calls for the sale of $50,000 in stocks. But, with this delaying tactic, only $12,500 or $15,000 in stocks would be sold in 1 or 2 days, and the balance would be sold in successive weeks in perhaps equal percentages. This defensive measure is based on the premise that a trend, once established, will continue in the same direction for some time, until it is offset by counterbalancing forces. If the trend continues upward after crossing the transfer point, more profit is realized on the subsequent sales than would have been realized if the complete action had taken place immediately.

Another delaying tactic, based on the same general premise as that described above, is the decision to alter proportions between bonds and stocks only at such specified intervals as 90 or 120 days. If a transfer point is crossed, any buying or selling action does not take place until the date of the next specified interval has been reached.

Still another delaying tactic makes use of some other method of trend detection. For instance, if the formula-plan schedule supplied a buy or sell signal, action might be delayed until a certain amount of movement had developed in the Federal Reserve Board Index of Industrial Production. The amount of movement might be a minimum number of actual-points fluctuation, or a certain minimum percentage movement. This use of the FRB Index, which was probably first suggested by H. G. Carpenter (2), is designed to prevent the purchase of stocks too early in a decline—at least to delay purchase until the FRB Index has begun to level out or turn upward. However, it is applicable only to declining markets, never to rising ones. Furthermore, the author feels that too much reliance should not be placed on the device. The consistency of relationship between the FRB Index and stock prices has not been sufficiently established in degree of amplitude of fluctuation, in parallel timing of turning points, or in regularity of movement in the same direction.

The introduction of defensive-action refinements might lay a variable-ratio plan open to the charge that too much judgment is permitted to enter; and we have seen that the elimination of judgment is one of the basic presumptions of formula plans. But experience has shown that these delaying tactics *do* work, and when one of the tactics—if not more than one—is combined with a well-conceived variable-ratio plan, the best net results are usually achieved.

Chapter 5

Practical Adaptations of Variable- Ratio Principles

The preceding chapter discussed and evaluated the major features of the variable-ratio idea as a basis for formula investing. The subject was handled largely on a theoretical level because the principal objective was to establish the basic operation of such a plan, as well as to give some indication of the diversity of development of the original idea. This chapter shows how the variable-ratio plan has been applied to the actual management of various institutional funds.[1] For convenience and for continuity with the preceding chapter, the funds selected for description are classified by the three principal methods for determining a trend line: the moving-average, the projected-trend, and the intrinsic-value methods.

[1] Material used in this chapter to explain the manner of operation of these various formula methods has originated chiefly from primary sources—from the institutions themselves which have sponsored these plans. Some of it has stemmed from correspondence of the author with the plans' operators, some from published brochures and other printed material which the sponsors have prepared to provide more public information about their methods. The published materials are listed in the bibliography.

MOVING-AVERAGE PLANS

The Vassar Plan

In 1938, the Vassar College Finance Committee adopted a variable-ratio plan as a guide to timing its investment decisions in the management of a part of the college's endowment fund.[2] The trend line was at the first determined by a 5-year moving average of the DJIA's mean annual high and low prices. Several changes were subsequently made by the committee in the method of constructing the trend. These changes, which are indicated later on in this section, were designed to provide a better guide to long-range stock-price value, as well as to provide what, in the opinion of the committee, was a more appropriate adjustment to changing economic conditions.

When the plan was initiated, the moving average established a price of 135 as a median level for the DJIA. With this as a starting point, the buying-and-selling schedules were set up as shown in Table 7. An inspection of these schedules reveals several important

TABLE 7. THE VASSAR PLAN, BUYING AND SELLING SCHEDULES

BUYING		SELLING	
Price	Stock/bond ratio	Price	Stock/bond ratio
135	50/50	135	50/50
125	66.7/33.3	150	37.5/62.5
115	83.3/16.7	165	25/75
105	100/0	180	12.5/87.5
		195	0/100

SOURCE: Reference 3.

points. In the first place, the fund was permitted to increase the aggressive portion of the account to 100 per cent on the downside and, similarly, the defensive portion to 100 per cent on the upside. If either of these upper or lower limits had been exceeded by the

[2] Background material on this plan and especially the recent changes which have led to the currrent attitude of Vassar toward formula operation has been derived from personal correspondence of the author with Mr. Francis Randolph, chairman of Vassar's Finance Committee.

subsequent price movement, the fund would have become temporarily immobilized and would have lost considerable flexibility to profit by a continuation of the price movement.

Secondly, on the buying side, only three purchase levels were provided below the median, while four selling levels were provided above the median. On the downside, the stock portion was increased at each buying level by one-sixth, or approximately 16 per cent; while on the upside, the stock portion was reduced at each selling level by one-eighth, or 12½ per cent. The reason for this difference in scale was not explained by Vassar when the plan was adopted. Perhaps it had something to do with the observation, from past price records of the DJIA, that it generally takes a longer time for the market to go up a certain distance than to go down the same distance, market drops often being quite sharp and abrupt. Therefore, more gain could, quite possibly, be realized by liquidating more slowly on the way up. However, the original schedule was later changed to equal numbers of buying-and-selling levels.

In the third place, the halfway rule was, in actual operation, employed as a delaying tactic. In obedience to the rule, no sales were ever made while the market was below the median and no purchases were made while the market was above the median. In other words, the delaying rule had the effect of postponing purchases and sales until the median had been crossed on the downside or upside, respectively.

The committee never completely eliminated the element of judgment from the conduct of its formula-plan operation; it felt that periodic reappraisal would be necessary because its plan was essentially a forecast of a certain amplitude of fluctuation. Because it was only that, it needed occasional review to determine if, in the light of changing economic conditions, the assumptions upon which it was based still warranted adherence to it. A formula plan that completely eliminated judgment over the longer term would, no doubt, in time find itself subject to a degree of rigidity that produced a more or less indefinite lack of adjustment to the current situation. Thus, if the buying-and-selling schedules illustrated above were in effect today, the Vassar fund would have been completely out of stocks (and immobilized 100 per cent in bonds) during the last 7 or so years. And, for this reason, the greater part of the current bull market in stocks would have been completely missed.

However, the committee saw fit, at times, to make certain revisions that, in its best judgment, made the plan more realistic. From a trend line based originally upon a 5-year moving average of the mean annual highs and lows of the DJIA, a shift was made in the early 1940's to a 10-year moving average. This gave a smoother trend—one less subject to cyclical fluctuations of its own. This line, with the same original upper and lower limits of 195 and 105 respectively, worked remarkably well during World War II market fluctuations. The fund became fully invested in stocks in early 1942—just a short time before the DJIA reached its low around 95—and it gradually divested itself of stocks in the ensuing years so that it became completely out of stocks (completely defensive) in early 1946—shortly before the DJIA reached its bull-market high of around 212. But Vassar's use of 100 per cent positions, both aggressive and defensive, has produced too much inflexibility whenever the market exceeded either of the outer limits. This has led observers to believe that it is better, under any kind of formula plan, never to be completely in or out of stocks and that some minimum stock or bond position (say, 10 or 20 per cent) is preferable as a sort of protection against the uncertainties of the future.

However, when the market broke in the fall of 1946 and continued generally depressed well into 1947, no occasion presented itself under the then-established buying schedule to replace the stocks that had been sold at substantially higher levels. The committee responded to the situation by deciding to revise the schedule and, in doing so, it raised the median level to 145 DJIA. While no stocks were to be purchased until that point was reached, successive buying levels were established at 10 per cent intervals on the downside, such as, for instance, 130, 117, and 105. Similarly, sales were also scheduled at 10 per cent intervals above 145, such as 160, 176, and 194. However, even this revised schedule did not provide a buying point in the next several years, as the low point reached by the DJIA in the erratic gyrations of the 1946–1949 markets was around 166–168. For this reason, in 1948, the moving-average method was given up entirely as a means of determining the trend. In its place, the committee installed an arithmetic-trend projection based upon a long-term chart of the DJIA from 1897 through 1947. In fitting an arithmetic-trend line to the basic cyclical fluctuations, the violent swings in prices during the 1927–1932 period were disregarded. In 1948–1949, this provided a median level of about 160 in the DJIA, a much more realistic situation. However, the almost steady rise in the Average since mid-1949, up to today's levels of around 500, again would have rendered the fund practically immobile.

Recent correspondence of the author with Mr. Francis F. Randolph, who is presently the Chairman of the Vassar Committee, reveals the committee's current thinking on the subject. Mr. Randolph says:

. . . the present policy of the College has not been adopted with rigidity but is subject to continuous review and examination by the Committee on Investments. At the present time, approximately 45 per cent of the consolidated investment fund of the College is invested in a diversified list of income-producing common stocks with the balance of the portfolio in governments, corporate bonds, and preferred stocks which are of sound investment quality and, on the whole, defensive in character. Under the existing longer term economic environment it is generally contemplated that common stocks will remain as a residual part of the portfolio.

To all intents and purposes, therefore, Vassar appears to have decided against continuing formula-plan operation except that the committee still abides by the general rule of selling stocks as prices rise and repurchasing as prices fall. But such action is now determined not by a rigid formula plan but, rather, by specific committee action. Mr. Randolph says further:

Generally speaking, it has been the view of the Committee that any rigid formula or other plan should not be adopted, in the light of the extraordinary factors which have operated in the United States over the last ten years. A revaluation of all the factors seems necessary from time to time and a course of action followed in accordance with the best judgment of the group and its investment counsellor has seemed the wisest procedure. This, of course, involves much deeper study and greater worry on the part of the Committee, but thus far, as I have said, it has proved advantageous.

The duPont Institutional Plan

The variable-ratio plan developed by the New York Stock Exchange firm of Francis I. duPont & Co. was first made available to the investing public in 1947. The duPont company is accustomed to provide as wide a variety of services and benefits to its clients as is possible, and the original research in the development of its plan was largely inspired by the firm's desire to make available, primarily to its institutional clients, a regular plan for the sound and conservative management of a large fund. The duPont Institutional Plan was, therefore, originally proposed as a sample of what might be achieved through the prudent management, on a formula basis, of an institutional account. (21)

Under this plan, the trend line is based on a 10-year moving average of the monthly mean prices of the DJIA.[3] This in effect amounts to a 120-month moving average. In developing their plan, the duPont people used data from 1895 to the then-current year and, on that basis, constructed a continuous 120-month moving average. This has been carried forward to the present time. The duPont firm is willing to accept its trend line as a normal price level because it is constructed out of, and in fact determined by, actual prices themselves: whichever way actual prices go, the trend will ultimately follow in the same direction.[4] The

[3] A monthly mean price is computed by taking the highest intraday price reached by the Average during the month, adding to it the lowest intraday price and dividing the total by 2. The average is then calculated by adding together the mean prices for the preceding 120 months and dividing the total by 120. The result is the current monthly trend value. This figure is not centered at the sixtieth month but is carried forward to coincide with the actual current data. Centering the trend value, however, would be the more correct procedure statistically.

[4] Some of the practical difficulties connected with the use of moving averages will be discussed in Chapter 8.

firm feels that a sufficient number of periods enter into the calculation of its moving average, and it is willing to place confidence in it as a reasonably proper index of normal value. It feels, therefore, that a forecast of the future direction or amplitude of stock prices is unnecessary and that a considerable amount of judgment can so be eliminated.

As we have seen, the trend line determines where a 50/50 stock/bond proportion will be established. When fund management under this variable-ratio plan is initiated, and the actual price corresponds exactly to the moving-average price, the fund begins with 50 per cent in stocks and 50 per cent in bonds. This state of affairs is assumed in the following discussion of the duPont procedure in setting up buying-and-selling schedules and determining transfer points. Unlike the original Vassar Plan, there is here no maximum or minimum for either bonds or stocks: the plan could *not* become fully invested in bonds after a market rise or fully invested in stocks after a fall, and the corresponding dangers of immobilization and lengthy periods of inactivity are thus considerably reduced. Transfer points are separated by 10 per cent intervals; the amount of the transfer effected is also fixed at 10 per cent of the *preceding proportion*. Table 8 illustrates this point; the market rises from a hypothetical normal or median level (200 DJIA) and the stock portion is gradually reduced. Action takes place whenever the market rises by a multiple of 10 per cent *of the median;* and, at each transfer point, the stock portion is reduced by 10 per cent of the current, *not* the in-

TABLE 8. THE duPONT INSTITUTIONAL PLAN,
SELLING SCHEDULE

DJIA	TRANSFER POINTS *Per cent of median*	STOCK/BOND RATIO
200	100	50/50
220	110	45/55
240	120	40.5/59.5
260	130	36.4/63.6
280	140	32.8/67.2
300	150	29.5/70.5
320	160	26.5/73.5

itial, investment. Thus no matter how high the market rises, the fund will never be out of stocks completely, for each successive reduction is progressively smaller in dollar amount.

TABLE 9. THE duPONT INSTITUTIONAL PLAN,
BUYING SCHEDULE

DJIA	TRANSFER POINTS Per cent of median	STOCK/BOND RATIO
200	100.0	50/50
182	90.9	55/45
167	83.3	59.5/40.5
154	76.9	63.6/36.4
143	71.4	67.2/32.8
133	66.6	70.5/29.5
125	62.5	73.5/26.5

Table 9 illustrates how the buying schedule is set up. Here the pattern of action of the selling schedule is repeated at each successive 10 per cent drop below the median, the bond portion being successively reduced by 10 per cent of its preceding level and the proceeds being used to build up the stock portion. The fund could never be completely invested in stocks because each transfer, while a constant percentage, is a progressively smaller absolute amount. This is to say that the actual dollar amount of stocks or bonds transferred will decrease as the distance between price level and median increases. The duPont firm presumably believes that, with a continuation of a price movement, the "pull" of the median on the price level will become greater, after the fashion of a stretched coil spring.

In the buying schedule of Table 9, it will be noticed that the transfer points below the median differ from those above the median (Table 8). Here the duPont firm has used a device it calls "percentage equivalents" to equalize action on both sides of the median.

In the actual operation of the plan, the halfway rule is employed, as it was under the original Vassar Plan. If the market is in a rising phase but is still below the median, no sales are made until the median is crossed; and conversely, if the market is in a falling phase, no purchases are made while the market is above the median. This is a delaying tactic that can yield more potential gain if the type of fluctuation is just right. If fluctuations are wide enough to cross the median each time, more gain will be realized by observing the rule than not; but if the fluctuations are not so wide, many profitable intermediate movements will have to be forgone.

In addition to the halfway rule, this plan embodies another type of delaying tactic that is designed to take greater advantage of a price movement once it has gathered sufficient momentum in either direction. The tactic, the duPont firm says, is based on a careful study of price records that reveals that, if the market as represented by the DJIA declines in a certain month, there is almost a 2 to 1 chance that it will decline further in the following month. The rule, then, provides for the following action:

Falling Market. If a transfer point calling for additional purchases of stock is reached, the purchases are delayed until the actual monthly mean price of the DJIA rises, in any one month, above the mean price for the preceding month. (That is, if the market continues to fall after a transfer point is reached, additional stock purchases can be made at more advantageous levels than if they were made immediately at the transfer point.)

Rising Market. If a transfer point calling for additional sales of stock is reached, the sales are delayed until the actual monthly mean price of the DJIA falls, in any one month, below the mean price for the preceding month.

Figure 2 shows how the duPont Institutional Plan would have operated from 1895 through 1954 with an initial fund of $1,000,000. By consistently applying the mechanical rules under which the duPont plan operates, the fund would have appreciated to a value of almost $10,000,000 by the end of 1954.[5] Moreover,

---

[5] Note that the DJIA increased about 12 times during the period while the duPont fund increased only 10 times. However, it must be remembered that the fund consisted at all times of both aggressive and defensive portions in varying percentages, while the DJIA is entirely aggressive. Also, hindsight does not indicate the real answer, which is really what one would have done at all times in the past, not what one would have done by looking back at things. The fund gave the investor a considerable measure of protection against the risks present in each past time period.

this satisfactory record of accomplishment would have been produced without the reinvestment of any of the current income. The upper half of the chart contrasts the performance of the fund with the record of the DJIA, the dotted line in conjunction with the Average representing the 10-year (120-month) moving average of its monthly mean prices. The middle section shows the continuous relationship of the monthly mean price of the DJIA to the 10-year average, reflecting the varying percentage monthly deviations above and below normal. The lower section shows the changing proportions of the total fund that would have been represented by common stocks at the time of each of the adjustments throughout the 59-year period.

The duPont firm takes justifiable pride in the results achieved through the operation of its Institutional Index. Figure 1 not only reveals the practical potentialities inherent in such a program but also demonstrates that the application of certain logical investment principles can prove rewarding in the long run without involving periodic forecasts of stock prices or necessarily assuming that future fluctuations will follow the same pattern they have in the past. As the duPont firm points out, in its prepared brochure on this plan,

the purpose of the duPont Institutional Investment Index is not to point the way to maximum speculative profits, but rather to demonstrate the possibility of using common stocks in an institutional investment program in such a way as to obtain better results over a period of years than could be obtained from fixed income securities alone. (21)

PROJECTED-TREND PLANS

THE KEYSTONE SEVEN-STEP PLAN

Perhaps the best known of the variable-ratio plans employing the projected-trend method of trend-line determination is the Keystone Seven-Step Plan. (22, 37) This plan was developed and is now sponsored by the Keystone Company of Boston, an invest-

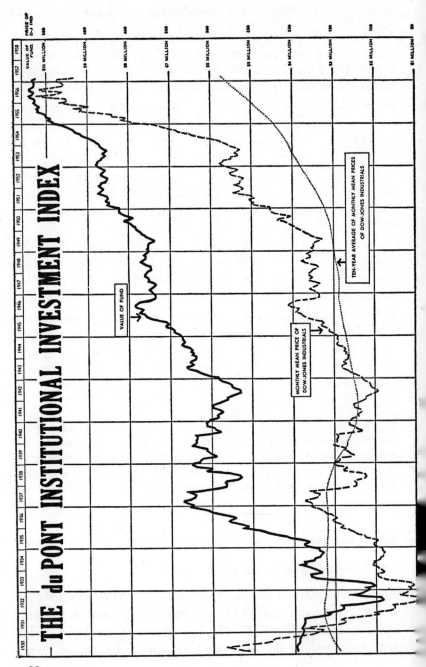

THE du PONT INSTITUTIONAL INVESTMENT INDEX

VALUE OF FUND

MONTHLY MEAN PRICE OF
DOW-JONES INDUSTRIALS

TEN-YEAR AVERAGE OF MONTHLY MEAN PRICES
OF DOW-JONES INDUSTRIALS

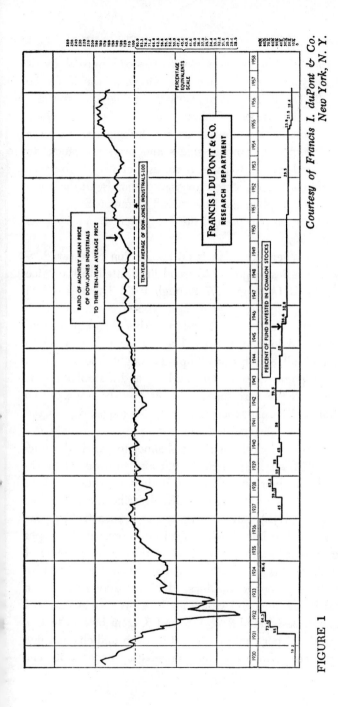

Courtesy of Francis I. duPont & Co.
New York, N. Y.

FIGURE 1

81

ment organization that manages various open-end mutual funds that are commonly grouped together and known as the Keystone Custodian Funds. The individual funds range in degree of speculative risk from the Low-priced Common Stock Fund, S-4, which consists of very volatile common stocks, up through several more conservative selections of common stocks and preferred stocks to an Investment Bond Fund, B-1, which consists of very high-grade corporate bonds plus United States government bonds. In the operation of the seven-step plan, the Low-priced Common Stock Fund serves as the aggressive portion and the Investment Bond Fund as the defensive portion.

Basically, the seven-step plan is an application of a variable-ratio formula to a series of projected trend lines fitted to the price movements of the DJIA from 1897 through 1947. The DJIA data are plotted on a logarithmic or geometric type of chart, on which equal distances represent equal percentage rather than equal absolute movements, and long-term trend lines are manually fitted to the data. First of all, an upward sloping straight line is drawn through the high points of past bull markets, and a similar line is then drawn through the corresponding lows (see Figure 2). (To avoid distortion of the trend, the abnormal price movements of the 1927–1932 period are disregarded.) The two lines not only demarcate a fairly wide, long-term rising channel to which the fluctuation of the DJIA has been confined but also turn out to be remarkably parallel in their upward slope. If they are projected into the near future, they should, theoretically, describe the pattern of fluctuation that the DJIA can be expected to demonstrate in the course of time. The top line should, therefore, represent the upper limit and the bottom line the lower limit of the expected range of fluctuation. Within this major channel, the seven-step plan provides for the fitting of four minor lines, which are drawn parallel to the upper and lower lines and which mark off five zones of equal width. The zones, designated 2, 3, 4, 5, and 6, from bottom to top, are approximately 15 per cent apart, that is, each mid-channel line is about 15 per cent above the line immediately beneath it. The

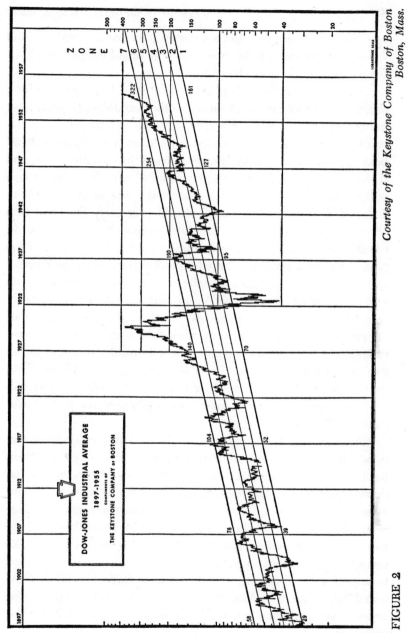

FIGURE 2

Courtesy of the Keystone Company of Boston
Boston, Mass.

83

two zones that complete the seven-step idea are designated 1 and 7; Zone 1 represents all the area below the broad channel and Zone 7 represents all the area above it.

It will be seen that this plan does not specifically provide for a single trend or mid-point, as do most other variable-ratio plans, but rather outlines a middle zone (Zone 4) in which a fund initiated according to the plan should be established on a 50/50 stock/bond basis. Then as the market advances upward through Zones 5, 6, and 7, the stock portion is progressively reduced and the bond portion built up; and conversely as the market declines through Zones 3, 2, and 1. If the price fluctuation should ever carry the DJIA into either Zone 7 or Zone 1, the fund would become frozen in the stock/bond ratio of the zone until a change in direction of the price movement provided for additional action. Thus, in Zones 7 and 1, the seven-step plan actually converts into a constant-ratio plan. This, however, does not mean that all action is necessarily ruled out, for some advantage may be taken of a continuation of the price movement—either upward or downward—by periodic re-valuation of the account and adjustment to restore the fund to the stock/bond ratio prescribed for the particular zone. Under these circumstances, however, while action is not entirely restricted, whatever action is possible can take advantage of the price movement to a limited degree only.

Actually, the seven-step plan is designed to provide the interested investor with several alternative degrees to which the stock portion should be reduced on the upside and increased on the downside. A somewhat conservative investor might prefer a bare minimum in stocks and a maximum in bonds whenever Zone 7 is reached; a somewhat liberal investor might be willing to hold relatively larger percentages in stocks at high market levels. The seven-step plan therefore sets up three alternative ratios designed to appeal to various ranges of investor preference. This is illustrated by Table 10, which shows the stock/bond ratios for the seven zones in conjunction with the actual price schedule for the year 1953.

TABLE 10.   THE KEYSTONE SEVEN-STEP PLAN

(Changes in stock/bond ratios under seven-zone operation)

ZONE	DJIA	Plan 1	STOCK/BOND RATIO Plan 2	Plan 3
7	304 and above	10/90	20/80	30/70
6	303–265	20/80	30/70	35/65
5	264–231	35/65	40/60	40/60
4	230–201	50/50	50/50	50/50
3	200–175	65/35	60/40	60/40
2	174–153	80/20	70/30	65/35
1	152 and below	90/10	80/20	70/30

Each year, the Keystone Company of Boston revises the DJIA price schedule to conform with the requirements imposed by the upward-sloping channel, which, it is presumed, will rise at a rate of about 3 per cent per year, the average from 1897 through 1947. As long as the rate of secular growth does not change, the seven-step plan might be expected to produce reasonably satisfactory results. But if the rate of growth changes or if the secular trend turns downward, serious problems will present themselves. An appraisal of the problem of a changing secular trend is considered in Chapter 8.

The seven-step plan provides for certain delaying tactics in its operation, and these have helped in the past to improve the actual results. One such rule that is carefully observed is the provision for rebalancing the account only at 3-month intervals. Thus if the price movement of the DJIA crosses from one zone to another— thereby calling for some change in the stock/bond relationship— action is not taken immediately but is delayed until the next quarterly review date. Provided there is considerable momentum behind the price movement, greater advantage will accrue to the fund if stocks do not have to be bought or sold on the same day that a zone line is crossed. Of course if the price movement reverses itself before the quarterly review date, the opportunity for realizing some capital gains will have been lost.

Another seven-step-plan delaying action that is regularly used is, essentially, a modification of the halfway rule. It was seen above that, if the plan were just being started and the DJIA price were in Zone 4, the fund would be initially established with a 50/50 stock/bond ratio. But once the plan is in actual operation, it calls for no rebalancing at all, on any quarterly review date, if the Average is in Zone 4. No matter whether the trend of prices is up or down, no action at all is taken until Zone 4 is crossed.

Now in Zones 1, 2, and 3, stocks are never sold, and in Zones 5, 6, and 7, stocks are never purchased. If, then, the DJIA is below Zone 4, any action toward rebalancing the account by selling stocks is delayed until the Average has moved through Zone 4 and into Zone 5. Conversely, if the DJIA is above Zone 4, any action toward rebalancing the account by purchasing stocks is delayed until the Average has again crossed Zone 4 and is in Zone 3.

The success of these tactics depends, of course, on a certain measure of momentum of the price movement. If there is sufficient momentum, more advantageous results will be realized by observing the rules; if there is little momentum, no rebalancing could take place. Thus, any potentially profitable minor movements would be missed entirely. However, the sponsors of the seven-step plan are reasonably satisfied with the way these rules have operated to maximize capital gain, for they have not yet had reason or occasion to modify them to any significant extent. It is, of course, possible that the actual price movement has fortunately been one that renders most effective the assumptions under which the rules were originally conceived. But if a future price pattern should lack some of the momentum of recent movements, and instead should fluctuate rather narrowly within Zone 4, the inactivity thereby imposed plus the inability to realize any gain whatsoever from minor price fluctuations might severely tax the investor's patience.

To bring the seven-step plan into perspective, Table 11 shows the Investment Timetable as determined by the Keystone Company for the year 1954 and the schedule applying to 1955. From the following comparison, it is apparent that the seven-step plan was then considerably out of step with the Average.

| YEAR | DJIA | | SEVEN-STEP PLAN | |
	High	Low	Zone 7	Zone 1
1954	404.39	279.87	312	156
1955	488.40	388.20	322	161

In this situation, actual portfolios operated under the plan would have been reduced to the minimum proportions in stock holdings. It is interesting to note that, up to the present time, the Keystone people have not seen fit to change their projected trend or to alter any of the basic principles that govern the plan's operation. Apparently their feeling has been that the DJIA has been in abnormally high ground and that a subsequent price decline will once more make the plan fully operative.

TABLE 11.   THE KEYSTONE SEVEN-STEP PLAN

(*Investment timetables for 1954 and 1955*)

| ZONE | DJIA | |
	1954	1955
7	312 and above	322 and above
6	311–273	321–281
5	272–238	280–245
4	237–207	244–213
3	206–180	212–186
2	179–157	185–162
1	156 and below	161 and below

NOTE: The proportions in which the fund is divided between aggressive and defensive securities for each of the seven zones are the same as those presented in Table 10 for each of the three types of plan available.

THE OBERLIN COLLEGE PLAN

In 1944, the Investment Committee of Oberlin College decided to apply the principle of formula planning to the management of the college's endowment fund. The plan adopted by the committee was devised, after considerable study and research, by Vincent S. Hart, Oberlin's Investment Executive. But although the committee was convinced of both the desirability of formula operation and the merit of the Hart approach, it prefers to maintain an open attitude toward its formula plan and likes to reserve to itself the privilege of initiating periodic revisions whenever conditions warrant. Certain revisions have already been made in the brief period of the plan's operation, and these will be discussed later in this chapter.

On the whole, the committee was initially quite satisfied not only with the results achieved by formula operation but also with the fact that its administrative procedure was considerably simplified and facilitated. Before adopting its formula plan, the committee would frequently find itself bogged down by the difficulties of reaching clear-cut decisions. The most formidable barrier to reaching unanimity of opinion had been the matter of timing; it had always seemed much easier to get general agreement on what to buy or sell than on when. By adopting its formula plan, the committee removed the question of timing from its agenda and so was able to devote almost undivided attention to security analysis and selection. The committee found itself to be more confident in its attitude toward equities even though, in the operation of its plan, it tried to retain as much flexibility and as much responsiveness to changing current conditions as possible.

Essentially, the Oberlin Plan is a variable-ratio formula based on an arithmetic-trend projection of the DJIA. The original basis for determining the trend was the DJIA data for the 1897–1925 period, but the plan was revised to use only the data for the 1910–1925 and 1934–1949 periods, thus eliminating the extreme price fluctuations that characterized the years 1926 through 1933. On the new basis, the trend has been calculated to rise at a steady annual rate of 2.77 points. But this annual point rise, it should be noted, becomes an increasingly smaller percentage of the market level as the DJIA continues to rise. This no doubt accounts for the fact that, in 1954, the Oberlin median was only 183 DJIA, as compared with a seven-step-plan median zone of 207–237, which was based on a geometric-trend projection. However, the committee is not particularly worried that its trend line may become unrealistic, for it is ready to modify the line whenever it appears inadequate to describe the current situation. It should be noted, though, that considerable danger may attach to a policy of frequent revision of the trend line. Such revision represents an intrusion of judgment and tends to nullify one of the chief objectives of formula plans: the elimination of judgment as much as possible. A more thorough evaluation of this point appears in Chapter 8.

As it was originally set up, the Oberlin Plan provided for a maximum of 65 per cent of the fund in stocks during a market decline below the norm or 50/50 point and a minimum of 25 per cent in stocks during a market rise above such point. Action points calling for rebalancing the account were spaced at 10 per cent intervals above and below the norm. Thus, each time the market advanced 10 per cent from the preceding level above the norm, the stock portion was progressively reduced; and each time the market declined 10 per cent below the norm, the stock portion was progressively increased. In a rising market, the stock portion was reduced by 3 per cent of the total fund with each 10 per cent rise until the 25 per cent minimum was reached. But in a falling market, the procedure was somewhat different. A distinguishing feature of the Oberlin Plan was the provision for purchasing stocks above the norm in a falling market: stocks were accumulated whenever the market declined from a higher level to a point that represented the fourth 10 per cent rise above the norm. From this point, the stock portion was increased by 3 per cent of the total fund with each successive 10 per cent fall until, when the norm was reached, the stock portion was increased by 6 per cent. After a 50/50 relationship was established, the stock portion was increased by 5 per cent with each successive 10 per cent fall until the 65 per cent maximum was reached.[6] These mechanics of operation can be followed

---

[6] The reason for these peculiar percentage adjustments on the downside has never been explained by the Oberlin committee. Perhaps it was the judgment of Mr. Hart that a slightly more accelerated rate of accumulation of stocks would be feasible as the median was approached and crossed on the way down. Yet there seems to be no statistical evidence to prove that this arrangement has any superiority over any alternative, more regular method of accumulation.

in Table 12, which shows the buying and selling schedules in terms of respective DJIA prices and the corresponding stock/bond proportions attained.

TABLE 12.   THE OBERLIN COLLEGE PLAN

(Buying and selling schedules and changes in stock/bond ratios for 1954 and 1955)

ACTION LEVEL		DJIA		STOCK/BOND RATIO	
		1954	1955	*Rising market*	*Falling market*
10	10% rise	474	484	25/75	
9	10% rise	431	440	25/75	
8	10% rise	392	400	25/75	
7	10% rise	357	363	28/72	
6	10% rise	324	330	32/68	
5	10% rise	295	300	35/65	
4	10% rise	268	272	38/62	32/68
3	10% rise	243	247	41/59	35/65
2	10% rise	221	225	44/56	38/62
1	10% rise	201	205	47/53	41/59
Norm		183	186	50/50	47/53
1	10% fall	165	167		50/50
2	10% fall	148	150		55/45
3	10% fall	133	135		60/40
4	10% fall	120	122		65/35
5	10% fall	108	110		65/35

Table 12 is interesting from several standpoints. One is the broad range within which the buying-and-selling schedule can effectively function without either becoming immobilized or converting necessarily to a constant-ratio plan. Thus, in the 1955 schedule, the point of maximum stock proportion below the norm (122) is 278 points below the point of minimum stock proportion above the norm (400). Based on the lowest level, this represents a range of fluctuation of approximately 230 per cent. Such a wide range for any one year is apt to encompass any degree of DJIA fluctuation. Moreover, considering the buying and selling schedules separately, the percentage range of fluctuation for the former is 123 per cent and for the latter, 115 per cent. Both ranges are much broader than are those of the other variable-ratio plans we have examined. Also, the Oberlin Plan is the only one thus far considered that would not have been rendered immobile by the DJIA's spectacular rise during the 1954–1955 period to levels around 450.

Another interesting point is the Oberlin modification of the halfway rule. In a rising market no purchases were ever made above the norm and, if the market was below the norm, sales of stocks were delayed until the norm was reached. However, in a falling market, provision was made for purchases while the market was above the norm but still falling. This unique provision obviously was but another attempt to incorporate a greater element of flexibility in the plan's operation. It would have advantageous results on those occasions when the market had dropped from higher levels but had not quite reached the norm. As a case in point, the DJIA declined from the highs of 1946, and the subsequent almost 3-year range of narrow fluctuation would have permitted some purchasing under this rule at prices that now appear to have been bargains. But to have waited for the norm to be crossed would have effectively ruled out many profitable buying opportunities. The Frontispiece provides a good perspective for this period.

Another type of delaying action that was generally, but not always, followed, depending upon the best judgment of the committee, was to buy or sell only a certain percentage of the amount called for when an action level was reached. For example, when an action point would call for a reduction in stocks by 3 per cent of the total fund, only a certain portion of that 3 per cent—say one-third or one-half—was sold at once and the balance was liquidated in ensuing weeks at perhaps more favorable levels, depending upon the degree of momentum of the current market movement. This tactic is similar to that which we have already examined under the duPont Institutional Plan. The latter plan is specific, however, in fixing the point of delayed transfer, whereas the Oberlin Plan seems to leave this to the discretion of the committee. This appears to the author to be a definite weakness of the Oberlin arrangement, for the more that judgment enters in, the greater is the departure from true formula operation, and perhaps also the greater the likelihood of error.

The initial few years of experience with its formula seemed to provide the Oberlin Investment Committee with a fair degree of satisfaction and generally greater confidence in its approach to its investment problem. However, the events of recent years have influenced the committee to depart more and more from the requirements that its formula would conventionally have imposed on its investment decisions. The long bull market that started in 1949 and reached new historical high levels in 1954 and 1955 would have caused the Oberlin formula to reduce stocks to a minimum proportion (25 per cent) when the DJIA had reached approximately 400. Thus, in the ensuing year, the fund would have become, in effect, a constant-ratio plan with no more than 25 per cent in aggressive securities. Perhaps a more sanguine attitude on the part of the committee toward the future course of stock prices, coupled with a growing disposition to enlarge the proportion of equity holdings that it is willing to maintain at all market levels, caused such a progressive departure from the original formula that it was given up entirely during 1955. Some influence in this direction may be attributable to changes in the composition of the committee itself—the introduction of members who did not have a part in the deliberations that produced the first formula plan and who therefore do not feel so obligated to abide by its dictates. Whether this committee decision to abandon the formula will later prove to have been the wisest procedure, or whether Oberlin will ever see fit to go back to its formula plan, cannot, of course, be known. At any rate, while any formula plan may make the investor disconsolate when markets are buoyant and prices are rising, a precipitate and extensive decline may provide sufficient reason for the Oberlin committee to reappraise formula-plan operation.

INTRINSIC-VALUE PLANS

The Birmingham Plan

The Birmingham Plan was conceived in 1946 by Mr. C. P. Heartburg, who was then the trust officer of the First National Bank of Birmingham, Alabama. At the time, he was enrolled in a course of study being offered by the Graduate School of Banking at Rutgers University, and, as the subject for the required thesis, he selected "Timing Common Stock Investment under the Prudent Man Rule." However, the subject was one that had long attracted Mr. Heartburg's interest and one on which he had done considerable thinking in an effort to achieve consistently better performance in the management of the trust funds under his supervision. He was trying to develop some method of determining "normal" value so that he could better estimate when stocks were overpriced and when they were underpriced. Based on a good deal of private research and painstaking observation of historical price records, he came to the conclusion that the market prices of stocks tended, in the long run, to fluctuate around their adjusted book values—at least, a sufficiently constant relationship seemed to exist to warrant further exploration. But the book value of a stock at each year end, when plotted on a chart along with the market-price fluctuations, would probably produce two separate lines which had no close chart relationship to each other. The usual concept of a trend is some kind of central-tendency line which more or less evenly cuts through the extreme highs and lows of the actual price data. The problem was how to bring the two series into closer correlation so that the book-value line might function reasonably well as a trend line. The answer lay in multiplying the annual book values by a constant—a selected figure determined by study of the past relationships between market price and book value. If, for instance, the market price of a stock tended to maintain an average level about 3 times book value in the past, we should, if we multiply the annual book values by 3, bring the book or intrinsic-value line into close adjustment with the price.

This is, in essence, the theory of this system. For use with a variable-ratio formula plan, however, the trend line is determined by (1) taking the book value of each of the 30 stocks comprising the DJIA, (2) multiplying each book value by a constant or factor that brings intrinsic value into line with market value, (3) totaling these adjusted book-value figures, and (4) dividing the total by the divisor used by Dow, Jones & Co., Inc. in the computation of its daily average figures. This adjusted composite book-value figure for the DJIA is then supposed to represent a reasonably accurate intrinsic-value trend line when plotted on a chart in conjunction with the actual price data. Adjustment is made semiannually, so that, in practice, changes in the trend line are never very far behind the changes that occur in the basic book values of the 30 stocks used in calculating the DJIA.

Under the Birmingham Plan, there is no one predetermined buying-and-selling schedule, because no one particular fund is being operated. Conceivably, a different schedule could apply to each of the trust funds administered by the bank. Whether the schedule is liberal or conservative and whether the maximum-minimum stock proportions are 100-0, 70-30, or 60-40 would depend largely on the particular needs and requirements of the fund and perhaps to some extent on the preferences of the trust fund's creator. However, the various funds in operation do attain some measure of uniformity by a provision for progressive reductions of 5 per cent in the stock portion above the trend line whenever a transfer point is reached and by a converse provision for progressive 5 per cent increases below the trend line. The only delaying action employed is the usual form of halfway rule: in a rising market purchases are not made above the trend line, nor are sales made below it in a falling market. Also, if the market is below the trend line but in a rising phase, sales are not made until the trend line is crossed; contrariwise, if the market is above the trend line but in a falling phase, purchases are not made until the trend line is crossed.

Although the Birmingham Plan, like all variable-ratio plans that use an intrinsic-value trend line, involves far too much computation and statistical analysis to suit the purposes of the average investor, the bank has been managing its trust funds on this basis for a period of approximately 10 years. The results actually achieved and the results of a test of the method with a hypothetical fund and the data of the 1926–1950 period seem not only to justify the effort involved but also to provide a measure of satisfaction that warrants continued use of the plan.[7]

THE CENTRAL-VALUE PLAN

The Central-value method of determining a trend line and subsequently basing a buying-and-selling schedule upon it was developed by Benjamin Graham, who offered it as a means of ensuring the selection of an intrinsic-value level that would be more realistic than that determined by other methods, would have the weight of logic and common sense behind it, and would conform more closely to the security analyst's usual conception of a proper approach to the basic problem of valuation. (9) Dr. Graham is inclined to prefer the capitalization-of-earnings approach to the problem of valuation. The mathematical computation involved in arriving at an approximate intrinsic valuation of a stock is reasonably simple —one merely divides the per-share earnings of a stock by an appropriate rate of capitalization. For example, if the per-share earnings of a stock are $3 and if it is decided to capitalize the earnings at 10 per cent, the stock's fair valuation is $30 (obtained by dividing 10 per cent into $3). But if this were all there were to the computation, it would be very simple indeed. Certain problems inevitably arise in connection with the choice of figures: What figure should be selected as reflecting typical or normal earning power? Should it be the most recent year's earnings; should it be an average of a number of years' past earnings, including both good and bad years; or should it try to take into account a projection of future earnings?

[7] Details of this test can be found in Cottle and Whitman. (4) In this test a comparison of results is made with the Central-value plan for the same period. From the standpoint of capital gain, the latter came out slightly ahead, when applied in each case to a hypothetical starting fund of $10,000.

A second problem is this: What is the proper rate of capitalization to apply to the earnings figure? This question is crucial, for a slight variation in the rate of capitalization could have a greater effect upon the final valuation than a similar variation in the earnings figure could have.

Fortunately, however, there are ways of resolving both of these difficulties. Most analysts seem to agree that the method of determining the earnings figure should largely depend on the nature of the past earnings record. If the net earnings have shown a steady annual upward climb, as is the case with many good public-utility stocks and if there is considerable evidence of stable growth, then the earnings figure would reasonably reflect *recent* earning power with perhaps some allowance for anticipated earnings growth. If, on the other hand, the past record of earnings is marked by rather violent fluctuations that have no pronounced or definite trend either way, then a reasonable figure would be an average of at least 10 or 12 years' earnings, including, if possible, as many good years as bad or, at least, one complete earnings cycle.

As for selecting the proper rate of capitalization to apply to the earnings figure, the generally accepted practice seems to be to make the rate proportional to the degree of business risk involved. Business risk may be defined as the extent or degree to which the earnings of a business enterprise tend to fluctuate. If it is estimated that there is a considerable degree of risk attached to a certain stock, it would probably be good judgment to select a rather high rate of capitalization, say 25 per cent; and conversely, if the risk is considered minimal, a low rate of capitalization should be selected, say 5 per cent. To illustrate how this would affect the final valuations reached under this method, let us assume that we have the common stocks of two different companies, each of which has average earnings of $3 a share.

STOCK	AVERAGE EARNINGS PER SHARE *Dollars*	RATE OF CAPITALIZATION *Per cent*	CAPITALIZED VALUE PER SHARE *Dollars*
A	3	5	60
B	3	25	12

In arriving at his Central-value trend line Dr. Graham employs a capitalization-of-earnings method that is essentially based upon the following assumptions:

1. The average earnings of the DJIA, as a unit, for the past 10 years are taken as a base to which is applied a rate of capitalization equal to twice the current yield on high-grade bonds. The resulting figure is supposed to represent a reasonably sound central, or intrinsic, value.

2. Whenever the DJIA declines to a point which is 80 per cent of the Central Value, or a distance of 20 per cent below the trend line, it would be sound practice to purchase common stocks. Conversely, whenever the DJIA advances to a point which is 120 per cent of the Central Value, or a distance of 20 per cent above the trend line, it would be sound practice to sell such stocks.

The high-grade bond index selected for use in this formula operation is Moody's Aaa Corporate Bond Yield Average. The yields on this index are computed currently by Moody's and the figures are published periodically. However, the actual earnings on the DJIA are not generally available for any one year until April of the following year. Therefore, to preserve consistency, the yield figure used is that shown by Moody's index for the month of April, when the DJIA earnings figure also is published. Table 13 shows how a schedule for the determination of Central Values and of buying and selling points is set up. The data are for the 10-year period of 1942 through 1951.

The Central-value formula has been computed back to the year 1924 and carried forward to the present time. A hypothetical test conducted to determine how the plan would have operated from the start showed highly satisfactory results. (4) Like most other formula plans it would have missed most of the spectacular rise in the market in 1928 and 1929, and it would have become fully committed too early in the decline to the lows of 1932 and 1933. But its record since then has warranted confidence in the fundamental

TABLE 13.   CALCULATION BY FORMULA OF THE CENTRAL
VALUE OF DJIA: 1942–1951

YEAR	AVERAGE EARNINGS TEN PREVIOUS YEARS	YIELD OF MOODY'S (Aaa) ALL CORP. BONDS APRIL, SAME YEAR	CENTRAL VALUE $\left(\dfrac{Avg.\ erngs.}{Twice\ int.\ rate} \right)$	CENTRAL VALUE		RANGE OF DJIA	
				80%	*120%*	*High*	*Low*
1942	$ 7.11	2.83	125.6	100.5	150.7	119.7	92.9
1943	8.08	2.76	146.4	117.1	175.7	145.8	119.3
1944	8.85	2.74	161.5	129.2	193.8	152.8	134.2
1945	9.46	2.61	181.2	145.0	217.5	195.8	151.4
1946	9.88	2.46	200.8	160.7	241.0	212.5	163.1
1947	10.24	2.53	202.4	161.9	242.8	186.9	163.2
1948	10.97	2.78	197.3	157.8	236.8	193.2	165.4
1949	12.58	2.70	233.0	186.4	279.6	200.5	161.6
1950	14.02	2.60	270.0	216.0	324.0	235.5	196.8
1951	15.97	2.87	278.0	222.0	334.0	276.4	239.0

SOURCE: B. Graham and D. L. Dodd, *Security Analysis*, 3d ed., McGraw-
Hill Book Company, Inc., New York, 1951.

soundness of the method. The one major deficiency in the pattern
was a failure to signal a sale of stocks in 1946. Of this failure, Dr.
Graham has the following comment to make:

It happens that the Dow-Jones Average failed to rise as much in 1942–46
as the stock market generally. Had the investor been guided by the
Standard Statistics Index covering 354 industrial stocks, he might actually
have sold out in 1946. This observation indicates that techniques can
always be improved by the application of hindsight. (9)

Dr. Graham further indicates that it may be possible that the
1946 market did not really complete its full rise in that year and
that the 1946 sell-off may have represented only a temporary interruption of a longer-term bull phase. At least, the market events of
recent years seem to be bearing out this prophecy.

It must be recognized, of course, that there is always the
possibility of a divergence developing between the Central-value
computations and the actual market prices of the DJIA. Calculation of the Central-value trend involves two independent variables:
earning power and the yield on high-grade bonds. Divergence is

not likely to come so much from the earnings factor as from the yield factor. Manipulation of interest rates by the monetary authorities, either to suppress inflation or to reinforce government fiscal policy, will cause high-grade bond yields to fluctuate. An earnings increase, which might justify a higher stock-price level, might be more than offset, as far as the Central-value line goes, by a rise in bond yields. Suppose, for instance, that we had the following hypothetical situation:

YEAR	10-YEAR AVERAGE EARNINGS	HIGH-GRADE BOND YIELD	CENTRAL VALUE $\left(\dfrac{Average\ Earnings}{Twice\ interest\ rate} \right)$
1st	$20	2.5%	$400
2nd	22	3.0	367

It must be recognized that a divergence is possible. Although it is not likely to be of long duration, it might result in a temporarily distorted Central Value and, consequently, in the selection of unrealistic buying-and-selling points. If, based on the earnings increase, the market happened to be rising at the time, the use of a level 20 per cent above the distorted trend as a transfer point might result in liquidation of stocks too early in the rise. This possibility does not necessarily invalidate the theory on which the construction of the Central-value line is based, but it is one of which the investor should be aware. A good, long-term comparison of stock yields versus bond yields for the 1906–1956 period is supplied by Figure 3.

Best results from the Central-value Plan usually accrue from an investor's buying and selling some or all of the stocks contained in the DJIA. If the investor prefers to use different stocks, perhaps those more volatile in movement, he should make sure that their fluctuations are more or less in line with those of the stocks used in computing the DJIA. If they are not, his buying and selling points might be poorly timed. If the stocks in which he prefers to deal have a tendency to exhibit fluctuations of their own, there is no inherent objection, of course, to his computing a central-value

line of his own. Another possible modification—one that might be
capable of very productive results—is the application of a variable-
ratio buying-and-selling schedule to the Central-value line. The
Graham method merely buys whenever stocks are selling at a level
that is 20 per cent below the Central Value, and sells whenever
they are priced 20 per cent above. No attempt is made to scale
buying down or to scale selling up. It would be a very simple matter to work out a variable-ratio schedule, while retaining the basic
Central-value concepts, so that stocks would be increased, say, 10
per cent with each successive 5 per cent decline below the median
and, similarly, reduced with each successive 5 per cent rise above
the median.

In concluding this discussion of Central Value, it is pertinent
to note a few things that Dr. Graham has to say about his own
method:

THE CLEVELAND TRUST COMPANY BUSINESS BULLETIN

Stock and Bond Yields Since 1949 the prices of common stocks have advanced faster than their dividends, so that the average yield has declined to a historically low point. Meanwhile the trend of bond yields has been upward from the very low level of the 1940s. As a result, the spread between the return on common stocks and on high-grade bonds was narrower in April than at any time in the past twenty years.

Changes in stock and bond yields beginning with 1906 are shown on the upper diagram. For stocks, the curve represents the average yield of all dividend-paying common stocks regularly traded on the New York Stock Exchange. The yield for any given month is obtained by dividing the sum of all the cash dividends paid per share during the latest 12 months, by the sum of all the prices. The curve for bonds represents the average yield to maturity of highest grade corporate bonds (A1+ rating), based on the index of Standard and Poor's Corporation.

The lower diagram shows the average yield of the common stocks as a multiple of the average yield of the bonds, with the series used being the same as in the upper chart. For any given month, the multiple is obtained by dividing the stock yield by the bond yield. Thus if the former is 6 percent, and the latter is 3 percent, the multiple is 2. On both diagrams the curves are plotted for the third month in each quarter. The figures for April, 1956, are indicated by the small circles at the right.

For April of 1956, the stock yield was 4.19 percent as compared with the 50-year average of 6.00 percent. The respective figures for the bond yield were 3.23 percent as against 4.07 percent. The table below gives comparisons by decades and for certain recent periods. The basic data are the same as on the diagrams.

	Yields on Common Stocks	Yields on Corp. Bonds (A1+)	Stock Yields as Multiples of Bond Yields
1906-15 Avg.	5.58%	4.65%	1.20
1916-25 Avg.	7.13	5.33	1.34
1926-35 Avg.	5.73	4.59	1.25
1936-45 Avg.	5.89	2.97	1.98
1946-55 Avg.	5.76	2.80	2.06
Year 1955	4.30	3.04	1.41
April, 1955	4.28	2.98	1.44
April, 1956	4.19	3.23	1.30
Avg. 1906-55	6.00	4.07	1.47

FIGURE 3

Our own experiments with this method have yielded interesting results on paper, but we hasten to warn our readers that they are not sufficiently dependable to warrant its use as a pattern for future operations. It would be surprising if it were otherwise. The investor has a right to expect good results to flow from a consistent and courageous application of the principle of buying after the market has declined substantially and selling after it has had a spectacular rise. But he cannot expect to reduce this principle to a simple and foolproof formula, with profits guaranteed and no anxious periods. (9)

We do not believe that they (results) can be projected into the future with any degree of confidence, or that they promise a sufficiently large gain to justify the risks they involve of "missing the market" and of losing

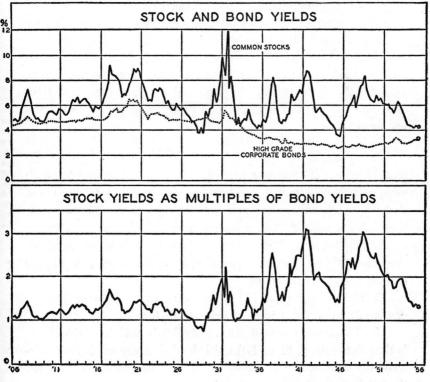

Courtesy of The Cleveland Trust Company
Cleveland, Ohio

investment income for a long period of time. These risks might make the enterprise an essentially speculative one, and apart from the mathematical probabilities of gain or loss, it would not be well suited to the psychology of the typical investor. (8)

THE GENSTEIN METHOD

For a number of years, Edgar S. Genstein, a New Jersey industrialist, engaged in private study that looked toward the development of a workable plan for his own investment guidance. The accumulated results and methodology were originally combined, in May, 1953, into a thesis for a graduate degree in Business Administration at Seton Hall University. From that time, the basic idea attracted sufficient interest that the author was encouraged to expand his original work into book form. (7)

The Genstein formula plan places primary emphasis on the dividend factor in the calculation of an intrinsic-value trend line, and the mechancis of the plan can best be understood if we first examine the manner in which the trend line is constructed. As the basis for the derivation of his price and dividend data, Mr. Genstein uses the DJIA. The calculation proceeds according to the following sequence:

1. An average price figure is calculated for the DJIA for the past 10 years. The average price for the DJIA is figured for each year, and 10 consecutive averages are then reduced to one figure that represents an average price for the 10-year period. In operation, this becomes a 10-year *moving* average of prices.

2. Dividends paid on DJIA stocks are similarly averaged for the same 10-year period. Operationally, this becomes a 10-year moving average of dividends.

3. The average price (1) is then divided by the average dividends (2) to obtain a ratio of price to dividends.

4. The current annual rate of dividends paid on DJIA stocks is then determined. Since DJIA dividend data are published quarterly, the current rate is simply the sum of the published data for the last four quarters.

5. The current annual rate of dividends (4) is multiplied by the ratio of average price to average dividends (3). This is supposed to provide a normal value of the DJIA for the current period, and these normal values constitute the Genstein trend line.

The next step is the determination of a buying-and-selling schedule above and below the trend line. According to the Genstein plan, a normal zone is established within which, apparently, neither buying nor selling takes place. The reasoning of the sponsor is that he is interested in finding out when stock prices (as represented by the DJIA) are in major accumulation or distribution zones, which are created by any *substantial* deviations of prices from the normal zone. The outer limits of the normal zone are determined as follows:

1. Buying starts whenever the DJIA reaches a level calculated as the normal value divided by 1.25. This in effect is a level which is 80 per cent of "normal." If, then, normal value were 300, buying on a scale-down would start at 240.

2. Selling starts whenever the DJIA reaches a level calculated as the normal value multiplied by 1.25. Thus selling starts at a level which is 125 per cent of "normal." If, then, the normal value were 300, selling on a scale-up would start at 375.

The following is an example of a buying-and-selling schedule that might be set up under the Genstein plan:

PRICE LEVEL *Per cent of Normal*	PERCENTAGE OF FUND HELD IN STOCK
145	10
140	20
135	30
130	40
125	50
Normal	50
80	50
77	60
74	70
71	80
69	90

Of course, the percentage intervals for gradually disposing of stocks on the way up and adding to them on the way down, outside the limits of the normal zone, could be narrowed or widened to satisfy the preferences of any investor. Also, interpolation could take place between the percentage levels if more frequent adjustments were preferred.

Mr. Genstein's hypothetical test of the past 20-year period reveals that, under his method, stocks would have been sold in 1938 with the DJIA at levels of 135–158, bought over the declining period of 1941–1942 with the DJIA at 115–95, and sold in 1945–1946 with the DJIA at levels of 175–212. (7) Also, his plan would have permitted purchases of stocks in 1949 when the DJIA was fluctuating in the rather narrow range of 180–163. This is a distinctly better showing for the 1946–1949 period than that of the plans examined above, which didn't provide for accumulation of stocks because the price movement had not declined to the calculated trend line. Moreover, at each of the buying and selling zones indicated above, the Genstein method would have permitted the percentage of the fund held in stocks to increase to approximately 80 in a buying zone and to decrease to approximately 20 in a selling zone.

The latest figure for normal, available to the author, under this method was approximately 320 for the DJIA in the second quarter of 1955. On this basis, selling would have begun as the DJIA advanced to levels above 400 (125 per cent of 320). At the peak of approximately 480 for the DJIA in September, 1955, the actual price would have stood at a figure of about 150 per cent of normal. At such a level, the fund would probably have been reduced to about 10 per cent in stocks. However, the extent to which dividends on the DJIA increased during 1955 would have had a correspondingly elevating effect on the trend line. The normal value currently is presumably higher than 320. If so, perhaps a slightly higher percentage than 10 might be maintained in stocks, probably something nearer 15.

There appears to be a considerable element of logic in the

dividend approach to trend-line construction. This opinion is shared by Cottle and Whitman, who state that:

although the *cyclical fluctuations* of stock prices and earnings appear to be more closely related than those for prices and dividends, the reverse is true of the *long-term growth* of prices. The authors' studies show clearly that the rate of secular growth of stock prices coincides closely with that of the long-term rate of increase in dividends. (4)

Further research on the subject may supplement the logic of the Genstein approach. However, Genstein relies on a 10-year average of dividends and a 10-year average of prices on the DJIA to provide a normal ratio as a multiplier of current annual dividends. Is a 10-year period the best one? Any other period would yield a different ratio and thus a different normal value. Perhaps research ought to develop along the lines of establishing a normal value that will, on the basis of past data, yield even better results.

Another criticism arises from the width of the normal zone. The higher the trend-line value becomes, the wider the normal zone becomes. In this zone (from 80 to 125 per cent of normal) no buying or selling is presumed to take place. But consider the effect of an approximate normal of 320: it would provide a zone with an upper limit of 400 and a lower limit of 256 DJIA. Within a range, then, of 144 points on the Average, the Genstein plan would provide no action at all. It is entirely possible that many sizable intermediate fluctuations could take place within the normal zone, without calling for any action under the plan. If the amplitude of fluctuation narrows down in the future, these potentially very profitable opportunities will have to be forgone. Of course, the trend line tends to be self-adjusting, which might have the effect of limiting the number of occasions of missing profitable intermediate movements that otherwise might have been entirely within the normal zone.

Chapter 6

Formula Planning for the Small Investor

To this point, we have been primarily concerned with the description and evaluation of certain types of formula plan that are particularly adapted to the needs of the large investor, such as the institutional fund, the investment trust, the insurance company, and the large private portfolio. It is the purpose of this chapter to consider the following questions: Can formula-plan principles also be applied to the requirements of the small investor? To what extent can the small investor answer his problem of proper timing by using a formula plan?

If formula plans were restricted merely to the large fund, their acceptability and hence also their potential appeal to the average investor would be seriously impaired. Any discussion of formula planning would then be necessarily confined to the needs of a very specialized audience. However, certain attempts have been made to embody formula principles in an investment program for the average individual and it is proposed to describe and examine these methods critically and to distinguish any significant differences in operational technique from the more conventional plans to which we have been heretofore devoting our attention. The central idea of these methods is the adaptation of formula principles to an *individual* stock. Buying and selling points are then based on the price fluctuations of the stock selected, rather than on the fluctuations of a market average, as we have seen was generally the method used in variable-ratio plans.

Of course, it is not intended to convey to the reader the impression that the equalization plans (constant-dollar, constant-ratio) and variable-ratio plans can not be adapted to the needs of the average individual investor. A great deal depends on the relative size of the fund he has available, on his psychological make-up, on his investment knowledge and experience, as well as on the amount of individual effort he is willing to put forth to devise and operate a plan in accordance with his needs. Perhaps he might gain the same relative advantages from the operation of a constant-dollar or constant-ratio plan as would a larger fund. At least such a plan is simple to understand, and easy to operate. Or he might with a little more patience and perseverance adopt some variety of variable-ratio formula which in his opinion might adequately suit his needs. In considering the following plans, therefore, the reader must bear in mind that they are but additional variations of the basic formula idea, which is to sell on a scale-up and buy on a scale-down, and that they have been conceived and adapted by their respective sponsors primarily for the requirements of the individual, and not the institution.

No claim is made that the plans herein described represent an all-inclusive presentation of the subject, or that other variations are not also in use privately by various investment counselors or individuals. But the three plans which follow are, at least, three of the better known plans in current operation and it is hoped that their inclusion in this study will help to provide a better appreciation of the almost infinite variety of which the basic formula principle is possible in practical application to differing needs.

Let us look first at the Burlingame Plan and the mechanics of its operation.

THE BURLINGAME PLAN

The Burlingame Plan[1] has been in continuous operation for over twenty years and is reliably believed to be the oldest investment program to warrant the name "formula plan." Its operation today is essentially the same as it was when the plan was originally developed—a remarkable fact that such a plan could withstand every vicissitude of the stock market the past twenty years, without any significant change in its details. It is also remarkable that the plan has been applied, at various times, to over 250 different stocks listed on the New York Stock Exchange without producing any disappointing results.

The Burlingame Plan deals with individual stocks; it bases buying-and-selling points on the fluctuations of the selected stocks, rather than on the movements of a recognized stock market average. For the individual investor, this may be more advantageous than otherwise. The only requirement is that the stocks selected fluctuate in price. And, if they do so in sufficient degree to test the plan thoroughly, the total of points fluctuation in several individual stocks is always greater than the total of points fluctuation in an average of such stocks.

Each individual, selected stock, then, may be said to have its own formula plan. After many years of careful research into the past price records of individual stocks, Burlingame has developed certain mathematical rules and tables. These are designed to provide the means of determining buying-and-selling schedules that attempt to maximize potential capital gain from each stock's price fluctuation. In the practical operation of the plan, these two objectives are always kept paramount:

[1] This plan was conceived and developed by Mr. Warren F. Burlingame, who directs an investment counseling firm under the name of The Burlingame Plan, 236 Huntington Ave., Boston, Mass. The term "formula plan," as it is applied to investment problems, appears to have originated with Mr. Burlingame, since the U.S. Patent Office has seen fit to grant him a trade-mark to use the designation "Formula Plan" in connection with his operations.

1. To minimize shrinkage of capital values due to a security-price decline.

2. To maximize the realization of (or at least to guarantee the greatest protection to) paper profits before a price decline wipes them out.

The first objective is achieved by committing at any one time not more than one-fourth of any fund allocated to a particular stock. By this means, three-fourths of the fund is kept in cash reserve to make possible additional purchases of shares at lower prices, should a price decline develop. At any subsequent purchase point, however, not more than one-fourth of the fund is committed. The second objective is achieved by entering protective stop-loss selling orders after a price rise has taken place.[2] That is, if a decline follows a price rise, most of the profit is protected by having the protective stop-loss order executed; on the other hand, if a further rise takes place, the protective stop-loss order is moved successively higher.

The mechanics of the Burlingame Plan can best be described by means of a concrete example. The capital fund allocated to a particular stock under this plan is usually either $4000 or $5000; rarely more than $5000. To facilitate computation, let us assume that a fund of $4000 is initially allocated. Let us further assume that, on the basis of the historical price record of the stock in which we will begin operations and the mathematical rules evolved from the record, additional purchases will be made at 20 per cent intervals from the starting price. We are now ready to operate. Let us consider two phases: (1) the plan in a price decline, and (2) the plan in a price advance.

---

[2] A stop-loss order is one given to a broker to protect a profit in a speculative position, and it does not become effective until a related transaction has taken place. If an investor bought 100 shares of a stock at $50 per share and the price later appreciated to $60, he could protect half of his profit by entering a stop-loss order at $55. Then if the price later declined to $55, the stop-loss order would be immediately executed at the best bid price that was available.

OPERATION IN A PRICE DECLINE

Having selected the stock in which we are going to operate, we will initially commit to its purchase one-fourth of the original fund, or $1000. If the starting price is 40, and if we disregard brokerage commissions and odd-lot fees, we will, then, purchase 25 shares. Another buy order is immediately entered at 20 per cent below 40, and the second $1000 is committed for the purchase of 31 shares at 32. If this order is subsequently executed, an order to buy 38 shares at 26 is entered, thus committing another $1000. If the price decline continues and the order is executed, the remaining $1000 is committed by entering an order to buy 47 shares at 21. If this order too should be executed, the fund will be entirely invested and a total of 141 shares will have been acquired at an average cost of approximately $28 per share. If the entire fund had been committed at 40, only 100 shares could have been acquired, and the unrealized loss with the price at 21 would be $1900, as against $1039 under this plan of accumulation.

Now, suppose a further price decline takes place below the figure of $21 per share. Here the plan introduces a novel feature, which, in this author's opinion, is unique in formula-plan operation. If the fund is entirely committed, how can it capitalize on a further price decline without bringing in additional funds or borrowing any money? The answer is this: After the purchase of the last increment of 47 shares at 21, a new stop-loss order is entered to *sell* one-fourth of the acquired shares at a price 20 per cent below the last purchase price. In this case, the order would be to sell 35 shares at approximately 16¾. The order, if executed, would yield cash proceeds of $586. Then, if there were a further price decline, the account would be in a position to buy more shares at lower prices. As a practical matter, an order would be entered to buy 44 shares at about 13¼, thus committing the $586. In the event of a decline to 13¼, the fund would have 150 shares, and the average cost would have been reduced to $26½ per share. This maneuver may seem to violate the basic formula-plan principle, which is to buy only on a scale-down and sell only on a scale-up, but it must be considered as protection against any steep and sharp price decline that takes place after the fund is entirely invested. If the decline goes far enough, the maneuver will release some funds for the purchase of additional shares at still lower prices. The move is supposed to provide some element of flexibility, yet the possibility of being whipsawed must not be overlooked, and the chance for loss seems to be as great as that for any additional gain.

The feature of selling a portion of the total acquired shares after buying on a scale-down and then reinvesting at a lower price is an integral and important part of the procedural operation of the Burlingame Plan. Moreover, the action can be taken any number of times that may be warranted by the price decline of a stock, each time further lowering the average cost and further increasing the total number of acquired shares.

In this particular illustration, two points are worthy of note. One is that, contrary to practice under other formula-plan operation, the defensive portion of the fund is kept only in cash, rather than invested in high-grade bonds or other less volatile securities. The other is that scale-down buying is done on an equal-percentage rather than equal-point basis. In our example we assumed the percentage to be 20, but it must be recognized that this applied only to the stock in which we were operating. For another stock with the same starting price, the percentage might be entirely different; and it might conceivably be different for the same stock at a later time and in a different price range. Thus varying percentages might be used at different times to determine relative buying points, and these percentages would be presumed to change as the price of a stock moves from a low to a high level and vice versa. The past record of price fluctuation would help to indicate when and how much to change the percentage.

OPERATION IN A PRICE ADVANCE

Most formula plans of the variable-ratio type attempt to set up some form of average value line at which the investment fund will be theoretically divided 50/50 between stocks and bonds. Above this line, no purchases ordinarily take place, since this is an area for scale-up selling, and contrariwise below the line. At this point the Burlingame Plan introduces another significant and novel departure from convention by permitting additional purchases as the price of a stock rises. Perhaps the intention is to give the operation greater flexibility, no matter which way the price moves. Since there is no trend line used with the plan, there is no way to detect when a stock is over- or undervalued. Hence the novel features, coupled with protective methods, give the appearance of some action either way. But it appears to the author that they are of doubtful validity and offer the investor as much chance for additional loss as for additional gain.

The mechanics of trading on the upside, the means by which profits are theoretically realized, and the means by which profits are protected against a subsequent price decline are illustrated in the following example. As in the example above, commitments are limited to one-fourth of the fund at any one time, the balance being held in cash.

Let us again assume our starting price is 40 and that we purchase 25 shares at that price, thus investing $1000, or one-fourth of the allocated fund. At the time of purchase, we have already seen that an order to purchase 31 shares at a price of 32 was immediately entered. At the same time, an order is also entered to purchase 20 shares at 48 on stop, a price 20 per cent above the previous commitment. Thus, the investor is in a position to take some action in the near future, no matter which way the price moves.

Now, let us suppose that the price rises to 48 and the purchase order for 20 shares is executed. But there is now a profit of 8 points on the 25 shares purchased at 40, and this profit should be protected. To do so, a stop-loss order might be entered at 45, which means that, if the price of the stock, after reaching 48, should suddenly decline through 45, our 25 shares will automatically be sold. Of course if the price keeps moving up, the stop-loss order price is correspondingly raised to protect as much of the profit on the original lot as possible. There is no definite, fixed-percentage rule that determines the price at which a profit-protecting stop-loss order should be entered, and the author considers this a definite weakness of the plan, since it introduces the necessity for a considerable amount of judgment. However, in actual practice, an attempt based on historical price studies is made to gauge the average magnitude of intermediate fluctuations of different stocks. But of course hindsight is frequently an unreliable guide to the future; in this case, it is just a guide and nothing more. There is an inherent weakness in this method that could expose the investor to needless risk. Historical price studies should never be wholly relied upon as a basis for action in an uncertain future. If there were no regularity of amplitude or period for intermediate fluctuations in the past, how can one expect any in the future? Moreover, an average of past fluctuations seems to be of no use whatsoever as a guide. In sum, the setting of stop-loss prices seems to be based on pure guesswork and nothing else.

Let us go back to the time when our second purchase order was executed at 48. All lots bought on the upside are considered entirely separate from each other. Thus when the purchase order of 20 shares is executed, 48 becomes a new starting price, and the previously entered order to buy 31 shares at 32 is automaticaly canceled. In its place, new orders are now entered to buy 26 shares at 38¼ on the downside and 17 shares at 57¾ on the upside. Then the cycle starts all over again. If subsequently the price should rise to 57¾ and the order to buy 17 shares is executed, then the order to buy 26 shares at 38¼ is canceled; a stop-loss order to sell 20 shares (bought at 48) is entered at perhaps 54; and new orders to buy are entered at prices approximately 20 per cent above and below 57¾, being careful in each case to limit each commitment to about $1000, or one-fourth of the fund.

Thus, the investor who operates under this plan makes no pretense of forecasting price movements. All he asks is that prices fluctuate, for whichever way they go, he is in a position to take some positive market action. He need never fear being caught fully invested at a market peak, for no more than 25 per cent of his fund could be invested at or near the high, and his profits on lots bought at lower prices would supposedly be protected against a price decline. He likewise need never fear being completely out of the market when it hits a bottom, for he will have been making periodic purchase on a scale-down and he will no doubt have invested some part of his funds at or near the bottom.

In the operation of the Burlingame Plan, a shift in investor psychology is necessarily imposed. Most investors are accustomed to buy fixed amounts of shares, usually round lots (100 shares) for varying amounts of money. A plan such as this one stresses the purchase of varying amounts of shares for fixed amounts of money. In this respect, the plan resembles some of the basic principles involved in the concept of dollar averaging. Trading is conducted almost invariably in odd lots. The investor may have some psychic prejudice against continuous odd-lot trading but he should remember that he is always guaranteed an execution at his price, assuming that a sufficient degree of price fluctuation does take place. Over a period of years the average annual return from operations under the Burlingame Plan comes out to about 8 per cent, of which about 3 per cent represents dividends and 5 per cent capital gains. To verify this, a study was conducted of the actual results on 57 different stocks during the period 1939-1944, and the average annual return, including both capital gain and dividends, was 8.3 per cent. (6)

The individual investor might be inclined to try this plan by himself in his own operations. But he would not have the benefit of the historical price studies and mathematical rules which The Burlingame Plan has developed. He might feel himself getting bogged down in a welter of computations, and he might also find difficulty in divorcing himself from his emotions: he might be reluctant to sell on an advance and afraid to buy on a decline. A more practical alternative, to overcome these difficulties, would be to authorize The Burlingame Plan to do it for him and to advise him periodically of buying and selling points. The rest is up to the investor. He uses his own broker; he can keep custody of his own securities, if he wishes; he is not required to engage in any short selling, or margin trading, since these practices are foreign to the plan.

For those who would like to follow through the operation of the Burlingame principles in actual market situations, two tables are presented. Table 14 shows how the plan operated in RCA common stock from 1943 through 1955; Table 15 shows operations in New York Central for a similar period. Data for these tables were supplied by The Burlingame Plan of Boston.

THE HOWE PLAN

Like the Burlingame Plan, the Howe Plan[3] deals in individual stocks and appeals primarily to the individual investor. However, there are certain significant differences in the operation of the two plans, and these will be indicated shortly. To facilitate an understanding of the Howe Plan, the basic principles as originally conceived will first be explained and certain of the revisions which are currently being embodied will then be indicated. The purpose of these revisions is to help to make the plan function better, to give it greater flexibility, and to adapt it better to meet the changing conditions of the market in recent years as well as the preferences and expectations of individual clients.

Fundamentally, the Howe Plan applies the variable-ratio technique to individual stocks. The historical price movements of the stocks that are selected for operations are carefully studied as a guide to the range of possible future fluctuations. An attempt is made to project, at least into the near-term future, the potential highs and lows of an individual stock. This is analogous to establishing the channel, or the upper and lower limits, of price fluctuation in the future, which, as we have seen, is such an important problem

[3] This plan was originated in the mid-1930's by Mr. Winthrop K. Howe, of the firm of Howe and Rusling, Inc., 183 Main St. East, Rochester, New York. From a personal conversation which this writer recently had with Mr. Howe, much of the detailed exposition above is derived, with particular reference to the major lines of modification which the original plan is currently undergoing.

TABLE 14. THE BURLINGAME PLAN

(Operation of the plan in Radio Corporation of America common stock with a $4000 fund)

DATE	SHARES BOUGHT	SHARES SOLD	SHARES HELD	PRICE	COST OF SHARES	SALE OF SHARES	PROFIT TAKEN	PROFITS (TOTAL)	SHARES (VALUE)	CASH IN RESERVE	TOTAL VALUE
6/23/43	89	..	89	11¼	1019.53	......	.....	.....	1001.25	2980.47	3981.72
6/19/45	71	..	160	14	1009.18	......	.....	.....	2240.00	1971.29	4211.29
6/20/45	..	89	71	13⅛	......	1147.56	128.03	128.03	931.88	2990.82	4050.73
11/29/45	58	..	129	17⅛	1006.15	......	.....	128.03	2209.13	1984.67	4321.83
12/12/45	..	71	58	18⅛	......	1269.52	260.34	388.37	1051.25	2993.85	4333.47
8/27/46	78	..	136	12⅝	1001.13	......	.....	388.37	1717.00	1992.72	4098.09
10/ 9/46	104	..	240	9⅜	990.30	......	.....	388.37	2250.00	1002.42	3640.79
6/17/48	66	..	306	15⅛	1015.30	......	.....	388.37	4628.25	–12.88	5003.74
6/21/48	..	80	226	14¼	......	1119.97	120.77	509.14	3248.00	986.31	4743.45
6/22/48	..	80	146	14⅛	......	1110.02	110.83	619.97	2042.25	1985.50	4647.72
6/23/48	..	80	66	14	......	1100.06	100.87	720.84	924.00	2984.70	4629.54
9/20/48	88	..	154	11¼	1008.08	......	.....	720.84	1732.50	1976.62	4429.96
2/14/50	64	..	218	15¾	1025.09	......	.....	720.84	3433.50	951.53	5105.87
2/17/50	..	77	141	15	......	1134.26	122.57	843.41	2115.00	1963.22	4921.63
2/20/50	..	77	64	14⅞	......	1124.68	112.99	956.40	934.50	2974.91	4865.81
3/30/50	52	..	116	19¼	1017.46	......	.....	956.40	2233.00	1957.45	5146.85
3/30/50	..	64	52	18⅛	......	1140.28	115.19	1071.59	942.50	2982.54	4896.63
4/18/50	43	..	95	23⅛	1010.76	......	.....	1071.59	2196.88	1971.78	5240.25
4/20/50	..	52	43	21⅞	......	1117.80	100.34	1171.93	940.63	2989.24	5108.80
7/10/50	58	..	101	17⅛	1009.94	......	.....	1171.93	1729.63	1979.30	4880.86
9/14/51	41	..	142	24	1000.17	......	.....	1171.93	3408.00	979.13	5559.06
10/20/51	..	50	92	22¼	......	1093.12	82.77	1254.80	2047.00	1989.48	5291.28
10/20/51	..	51	41	22¼	......	1115.17	104.82	1359.52	912.25	2999.83	5271.60
4/14/52	35	..	76	28⅞	1026.92	......	.....	1359.52	2194.50	1972.91	5526.93
4/15/52	..	41	35	27⅜	......	1103.55	103.38	1462.90	958.13	2973.08	5394.11

Date											
11/13/53	47	:	82	21%	1020.65	......	......	1462.90	1752.75	1952.43	5168.08
6/30/54	34	:	116	29%	1022.51	......	......	1462.90	3426.50	929.92	5819.32
8/30/54	:	82	34	31%	......	2548.67	501.10	1964.00	1071.00	2977.49	6012.49
11/ 5/54	28	:	62	35%	1015.84	......	......	1964.00	2216.50	1961.65	6142.15
11/15/54	:	34	28	36	......	1205.18	182.67	2146.67	1008.00	2984.16	6138.83
2/16/55	23	:	51	42%	997.61	......	......	2146.67	2180.25	1986.55	6313.47
2/25/55	:	28	23	42%	......	1172.12	156.28	2302.95	977.50	3002.39	6282.84
5/26/55	20	:	43	50%	1024.45	......	......	2302.95	2171.50	1977.94	6452.39
6/28/55	:	23	20	50%	......	1150.10	152.49	2455.44	1015.00	2975.55	6445.99

TABLE 15. THE BURLINGAME PLAN

(Operation of the plan in New York Central common stock with a $4000 fund)

DATE	SHARES BOUGHT	SHARES SOLD	SHARES HELD	PRICE	COST OF SHARES	SALE OF SHARES	PROFIT TAKEN	PROFITS (TOTAL)	SHARES (VALUE)	CASH IN RESERVE	TOTAL VALUE
10/ 4/39	48	..	48	20⅞	1013.52	......	.....	.....	1002.00	2986.48	3988.48
1/15/40	60	..	108	16¼	987.60	......	.....	.....	1755.00	1998.88	3753.88
5/14/40	78	..	186	12⅝	1001.13	......	.....	.....	2348.25	999.75	3348.00
5/21/40	98	..	284	10	1000.58	......	.....	.....	2840.00	–2.83	2837.17
4/ 7/43	..	95	189	18⅛	......	1698.06	363.78	363.78	3425.63	1331.35	5120.76
4/ 7/43	..	95	94	18	......	1686.21	351.93	715.71	1692.00	2665.63	5073.34
4/ 9/43	..	94	0	17⅜	......	1609.76	275.49	991.20	0.00	4000.00	4991.20
4/15/43	58	..	58	17¼	1013.15	......	.....	991.20	1000.50	2986.85	4978.55
3/22/44	48	..	106	20⅞	1013.39	......	.....	991.20	2212.75	1973.46	5177.41
3/23/44	..	58	48	19⅝	......	1123.48	110.33	1101.53	937.00	2986.61	5025.14
1/ 8/45	40	..	88	24⅞	1004.89	......	.....	1101.53	2189.00	1981.72	5272.25
1/15/45	..	48	40	24⅞	......	1180.18	166.79	1268.32	995.00	2995.11	5258.43
6/ 6/45	..	40	0	28	......	1108.17	103.28	1371.60	0.00	4000.00	5371.60
6/ 8/45	34	..	34	29⅛	999.02	......	.....	1371.60	990.25	3000.98	5362.83
12/19/45	29	..	63	34	993.83	......	.....	1371.60	2142.00	2007.15	5520.75
12/20/45	..	34	29	32½	......	1094.56	95.54	1467.14	942.00	3006.17	5415.31
5/ 9/46	40	..	69	25⅛	1014.91	......	.....	1467.14	1733.63	1991.26	5192.03
9/ 3/46	53	..	122	18⅝	988.87	......	.....	1467.14	2272.25	992.39	4738.78
5/13/47	71	..	193	13⅞	1000.02	......	.....	1467.14	2677.88	–7.63	4137.39
1/19/51	..	96	97	24½	......	2322.77	318.96	1786.10	2376.50	1996.18	6158.78
1/19/51	..	97	0	24⅝	......	2359.13	355.31	2141.41	0.00	4000.00	6141.41
1/23/51	41	..	41	24¼	1010.16	......	.....	2141.41	994.25	2989.84	6125.50
5/23/51	55	..	96	18	1006.16	......	.....	2141.41	1728.00	1983.68	5853.09
12/10/52	..	96	0	22⅛	......	2095.79	79.47	2220.88	0.00	4000.00	6220.88

for variable-ratio plans. What Howe is trying to do is to set up the long-term trend and its range as well as possible and then to profit from cyclical price fluctuations within that range.

Unlike the Burlingame Plan, the Howe Plan does not allocate a fixed dollar amount to any stock, for the latter plan can theoretically operate with whatever amount of capital the investor may have available. Again unlike the former plan, the Howe Plan does not keep the defensive portion of the fund in cash but, instead, invests it in high-grade bonds or other securities that are normally less susceptible to wide price fluctuation.

Once the expected high-to-low range is determined, the size of the initial commitment depends upon the relationship of the current price to the anticipated range. If, for instance, a certain stock could be expected to have a range in the foreseeable future of 40 to 100 and the current price happened to be 70, 50 per cent of the available fund would be invested in the stock and 50 per cent in bonds. If the current price were around 40, the fund would be entirely committed to the stock; if the price were 100, the fund would be kept entirely defensive. As prices declined below 70, the fund would become progressively more aggressive than defensive, and as prices advanced above 70, the fund would become progressively more defensive than aggressive. Thus, at 85, for instance, the fund might be divided 75 per cent defensive and 25 per cent aggressive, while at a price of 55, it might possibly be 25 per cent defensive and 75 per cent aggressive. While the proportions at any specific price do not necessarily have to be mathematically exact, they would probably tend to be so, at least for the initial commitment. It must be pointed out in this connection that considerably more personal judgment enters into the operation of the Howe Plan than some of the other plans we have been considering. The more that personal judgment enters, the further does a plan depart from the formula-plan concept. The author considers this a definite weakness of the Howe Plan, at least so far as classification goes. Formula plans of the more conventional type recognize that judgment is not infallible and therefore try to eliminate this potential source of error as much as possible.

The program just outlined, it must be remembered, determines just one thing: the size of the initial commitment. The initial purchase, once made, is subdivided into appropriate blocks that, if the price rises, are sold on a scale-up. If the price reaches the projected high, the last block is sold and the fund becomes entirely defensive. If, however, the price declines after the initial purchase, more blocks of stock are bought at specified transfer points. If the projected low is reached, the fund becomes entirely aggressive. Once the fund is entirely invested in stock, the number of acquired shares is again subdivided into blocks and these blocks are similarly liquidated on a scale-up, assuming a reversal of the price movement after the stock reaches its projected low point.

It should be helpful at this point to follow through a hypothetical example and to show how profits are realized after the stock undergoes a complete price cycle. It must be emphasized that Table 16 serves an illustrative purpose only and that the actual price movement in any individual case would not be so rhythmically perfect or correspond so exactly with the projected high and low points.

Let us assume an operating fund of $7000; an anticipated price range of 40–100; a current price of 70; and therefore an initial commitment of $3500, or the purchase of 50 shares at 70. In our illustra-

TABLE 16.   THE HOWE PLAN

(*Hypothetical operation of the plan over a complete price cycle*)

ACTION	PRICE	STOCK FUND	NO. OF SHARES	BOND FUND	TOTAL FUND	REAL-IZED PROFIT	REAL-IZED LOSS
Buy 50 shares	70	$3500	50	$3500	$7000		
Sell 20 shares	80	2400	30	5100	7500	$200	
Sell 20 shares	90	900	10	6900	7800	400	
Sell 10 shares	100	...	..	7900	7900	300	
Buy 20 shares (A)	85	1700	20	6200	7900		
Buy 30 shares (B)	70	3500	50	4100	7600		
Buy 50 shares (C)	50	5000	100	1600	6600		
Buy 40 shares (D)	40	5600	140	....	5600		
Sell 20 shares (1/2D)	50	6000	120	1000	7000	200	
Sell 20 shares (1/2D)	60	6000	100	2200	8200	400	
Sell 30 shares (3/5C)	70	4900	70	4300	9200	600	

tion we assume that the price of the stock first moves up to the projected high, then suffers a sharp decline to the projected low, and then recovers to the starting price of 70. A *buy-and-hold policy*— that is, buying 50 shares at 70 and holding them throughout the whole period of fluctuation—would show no profit at all after completion of the price cycle. The Howe Plan, however, shows realized profits of $2100 (which have been reinvested into the account) and a total fund value of $9200 as compared with an initial fund of $7000. Allowing fully for the unreality of our hypothetical example, some potential advantage does seem to accrue to an investor who uses this plan in preference to a buy-and-hold policy or some other program based on pure guesswork.

This plan does not involve the use of any stop-loss orders, nor does it provide for any margin trading. It also does not allow for any purchases on a scale-up, in contrast to the Burlingame Plan. Depending upon the manner in which the price of the stock happens to fluctuate, the size of the stock fund is either increased or decreased. Thus, if the price continues to rise, more blocks of shares are sold; if the price declines, more shares are purchased.

Under the Howe Plan, the defensive portion of the fund is not held continuously in cash but is customarily invested in securities that are relatively stable in price. Usually the primary reserve is divided into two parts: (1) securities such as high-grade bonds, generally U.S. Treasury issues, or investment-grade preferred stocks, and (2) carefully selected growth situations, whose long-term trend is considered to be upward, but whose short-term trend is not subject to much price variation. The sponsors of the Howe Plan prefer, for this second part, such issues as those of growing Western and Southwestern banks and growth utilities, some well-situated insurance stocks, and some carefully screened convertible bonds. In fact, convertible bonds seem to be growing in preference as a medium for employment of the second part of the primary reserve. If there were no value to the convertible feature, a convertible bond would sell on the same yield basis as that of other bonds of similar investment risk. Thus, a certain limit is placed on the extent of a price decline in this type of security. However, there is no limit on how *high* it can sell, for its market price will rise in direct proportion to the rise in the price of the common stock into which it is convertible. If all stocks fluctuated together, a policy of buying convertible bonds would be dangerous, for, as the aggressive portion of an investment fund was reduced during a price rise, the funds released would be committed to convertible issues precisely at a time when they too might be selling at their highest prices.

Not only does this policy provide for some current income on the defensive portion but it also may produce some capital gain whenever the aggressive portion is in the process of periodic reduction. In this respect some chief objections of the investor are answered concerning the unproductivity of the defensive fund, if such were maintained entirely in cash.

The Howe Plan sponsors are currently undertaking considerable study and research to introduce certain revisions that would make their plan more flexible and more adaptable to current conditions. They have become impressed with the fact that the frequency as well as the amplitude of intermediate fluctuations in post-World War II markets have been considerably reduced, and so also the opportunity to take advantage of short-term price fluctuations. They are therefore revising their price ranges as well as their buying-and-selling policies to make them more responsive to current conditions. Two chief factors are considered in revising the projected price range of a stock. One is the changing purchasing power of the dollar; the other is the change in the intrinsic-asset values of the stocks in which operations are conducted. The latter provides allowance for accelerated depreciation policies, greater reinvestment of earnings, and more conservative dividend policies. Thus, the projected price range of a stock is revised periodically to conform more adequately with changes in the basic-value determinants. Moreover, the price ranges of stocks of companies that are undergoing rapid growth are promptly revised to take into account the development of factors (such as new products, processes, markets, or expansion) that seem to point to extraordinary gains in earnings and asset values in the foreseeable future. This does not imply that study of the historical price record of a stock is disregarded as a guide to price-range projection, but rather that the projection is modified either upward or downward according to changes in basic values. Naturally, the objections will be raised that this policy departs more and more from the basic concept of a formula plan and that it necessarily implies the use of greater degrees of judgment, which is not always correct. The results under such a method will be good only to the extent that the judgment used is good; if poor judgment is used, the results will be correspondingly poor. The sponsors are apparently trying to reconcile a kind of formula-plan operation with the needs and desires of individual clients. Paying too much attention to the latter often results in very little being left of the former.

THE NEW ENGLAND PLAN

The New England Plan was originated in 1949 and put into operation by the Samuel S. Cadwell Co., Westport, Connecticut; it is more recent in origin than either the Howe or Burlingame plans. Like the others, it deals primarily in individual stocks and, in determining when stocks should be bought or sold and in what amounts, it employs basically the variable-ratio technique. It may be observed here that, in its operation, the New England Plan contains certain elements that characterize both the Howe and the Burlingame plans. These elements have been combined with certain concepts of the plan's sponsors into a synthesis of which the end result, it is claimed, is the achievement of greater flexibility. The elements of similarity will be indicated as the analysis of this plan proceeds.

The New England Plan has selected 41 common stocks, to which it applies its principles of operation. In the selection of these stocks, primary consideration was given to two criteria: (1) the quality of the issue, and (2) the regularity of fluctuation. In regard to the first criterion, the type of stock found to be most adaptable to operation was the blue-chip or market-leader type—generally a stock showing a long, consistent record of good earnings and regular dividends. In regard to the second criterion, regularity or consistency of fluctuation, as revealed by historical price studies, was found essential to selection. This was deemed more important than the size or amplitude of the fluctuation; since each individual stock may be said to have its own variable-ratio formula, the percentage differentials for the purchase of each issue are adjusted to provide due allowance for the size of the expected fluctuation. Thus, a stock subject to fairly wide price swings would have a considerably wider purchase schedule than a stock subject to fairly narrow price swings. On the face of it, it would appear that a stock with a high price volatility would offer more prospect for capital gain than would a stock that was less volatile but more regular in fluctuation. Yet a volatile stock may have very irregular, though sharp, movements, and so its profit-producing possibilities in the long run may actually turn out to be less than those of a stock with greater regularity of movement.

Like the Howe Plan, the New England Plan tries to determine a possible projected range of fluctuation for the future. But whereas the former relies on judgment based on historical price study, the latter employs a trend line calculated by taking a 10-year moving average of actual price fluctuations.[4] Once this line is determined, it is important next to establish an "expectable possible low" and an "expectable possible high" in relation to the trend. If the near-term price trend of the stock is up, these expectable lows and highs will be higher than those of the previous cycle, and vice versa.

The area between the expectable high and the expectable low is then divided into three zones. The middle zone is considered the normal zone, while the upper zone is above normal, and the lower zone below normal. These zones provide a guide for determining the amount of the initial purchase. The following schedule illustrates how the size of the initial purchase is determined, the percentages being those applicable to whatever fund is allocated to a particular issue.

---

[4] Some of the difficulties inherent in the use of the moving-average concept as a measure of "normal" value are pointed out in Chapter 8.

ZONE	PERCENTAGE OF FUND
Above normal	10
Normal	25
Below normal	40

These percentages, it must be emphasized, apply to the initial commitment only. Once that has been made, the percentage scale that is set up to provide for future purchases is determined by the relationship of the starting price to the expectable possible low. For example, if the starting price is in the above-normal zone, an initial commitment of only 10 per cent is made; if the price continues to rise, scale-up purchasing is permitted but is strictly limited to 10 per cent of the fund for each separate purchase.[5] With respect to allowing purchases on a scale-up, the New England Plan is similar to the Burlingame Plan, but it is much more precise and definite in the way in which it limits the size of the commitments and determines the price levels at which the commitments will be made. However, if the price declines after an initial 10 per cent purchase in the above-normal zone, subsequent commitments are increased to 20 per cent, then to 30 per cent, and finally to 40 per cent when the expectable possible low is reached. By this means, the fund can become completely invested in an individual stock.

If the starting price is in the normal zone, an initial commitment of 25 per cent of the fund is made and is followed by additional 25 per cent purchases as the price declines to the expectable possible low. Succeeding commitments are made at successively lower prices, each of which is spaced an equal percentage distance below the other, with the final 25 per cent of the fund being invested at the expectable low itself. Thus if the current price of a stock were 60 in the normal zone and the expectable possible low were 30, the scale of purchasing would be that of Table 17, assuming a $4000 fund.

The various purchase levels of Table 17 are approximately 20 per cent apart, and the end result of the program is the acquisition of 96 shares at an average price of 41½.

[5] This scale-up purchasing feature is subject to the same criticism as that made earlier of the Burlingame Plan.

TABLE 17. THE NEW ENGLAND PLAN

(*Sample purchase schedule starting from normal zone*)

PRICE	PERCENTAGE OF FUND	AMOUNT INVESTED	NUMBER OF SHARES
60	25	$1000	16
48	25	1000	21
38	25	1000	26
30	25	1000	33
	100	$4000	96

Average cost = 41½

If the starting price is in the below-normal zone, the initial commitment is 40 per cent of the fund. Additional purchases are then made in the proportions of 30, 20, and 10 per cent, with the last purchase being made at the expectable possible low. This scale is just the reverse of that used when the price of a stock declines after an initial purchase in the *above*-normal zone; in this case, the *smallest* dollar commitment is made when the price is at its *lowest*. This may seem peculiar because it seems to be a departure from more conventional formula procedure and also because it results in a somewhat higher average cost. The reasoning behind the procedure is based on the fact that, at the start, the price of the stock is already in the below-normal zone, where the initial commitment is largest. It is desirable, therefore, to accumulate as much stock as possible while the price is below normal, both because the trend may be reversed at any moment and because there is no definite assurance that the expectable possible low will ever be reached. The

TABLE 18. THE NEW ENGLAND PLAN

(*Sample purchase schedule starting from below-normal zone*)

PRICE	PERCENTAGE OF FUND	AMOUNT INVESTED	NUMBER OF SHARES
45	40	$1600	35
39½	30	1200	30
34¾	20	800	23
30	10	400	13
	100	$4000	101

Average cost = 39½

purchase schedule might look like that of Table 18, assuming a starting price of 45 (15 below normal), an expectable possible low of 30, a fund of $4000, and purchase levels approximately 12 per cent apart.

In our previous illustrations, we have seen how a fund invested under the New England Plan would become fully invested on a scale-down. But it has already been indicated that the plan also provides for scale-up purchases in order to make possible some positive market action whichever way the price happens to move. If, after the initial purchase is made, the price should rise rather than decline, a scale-up purchase schedule would also be established. Normally, scale-up purchases are made at intervals that are 60 per cent of those that separate purchases on the downside. Let us refer to our example of operation from the normal zone, when an initial commitment of 25 per cent of the fund of $4000 was made at a price of 60. On the downside, the purchase levels were spaced approximately 20 per cent apart. Therefore, on the upside, purchase levels would be spaced 12 per cent apart (60 per cent of 20). Thus, if the price began to rise from a starting point of 60, the purchase schedule would be that of Table 19.

TABLE 19.   THE NEW ENGLAND PLAN

(*Sample purchase schedule on scale-up*)

PRICE	PERCENTAGE OF FUND	AMOUNT INVESTED	NUMBER OF SHARES
60	25	$1000	16
67¼	25	1000	15
75⅜	25	1000	13
84½	25	1000	12
	100	$4000	56
Average cost = 71½			

In actual practice, once the initial purchase had been made, two additional purchase orders would be immediately entered: one for 15 shares at 67¼ on stop order and the other for 21 shares at 48. In this respect, the New England Plan is very similar to the Burlingame Plan; possibly the only difference lies in the fact that percentage purchase levels are more precisely determined by pre-established rules and are more rigidly observed.

The question now is the method of realizing profits under the New England Plan; the answer is the use of carefully placed stop-loss orders. The procedure of placing the stop-loss orders is slightly different in a declining market than it is in a rising market.

Declining Market. In the example of scale-down purchasing from a starting point in the normal zone, we saw that, when the expectable possible low was reached, the fund was fully invested, having acquired a total of 96 shares at an average cost of 41½. A stop-loss order is then entered as soon as the market price rises 12½ per cent above the average cost. The point at which it is entered is halfway between the average cost and the price that represents a 12½ per cent gain. In our example, a 12½ per cent gain over average cost can be had by selling at 46¾; the stop-loss-order price then would be 44⅛. The sell order would cover 75 per cent of the shares acquired; the other 25 per cent being retained to start a new plan at 44⅛. Thus, the sell order would be for 73 shares at 44⅛ stop (96 shares less the 23 at 44⅛ which would represent a new initial 25 per cent commitment). If, therefore, the market price reached the point of 12½ per cent gain over average cost and then so declined that the stop-loss order was executed, 73 shares would be sold at a profit of slightly over $191. If the price continued to rise, the stop-loss-order price would be continuously advanced, a new stop-loss order being entered each time the stock recorded a 12½ per cent gain from the previous level.

Rising Market. If the purchases have been made on a scale-up, some profit on the earlier lots has already accrued and should be protected. The point of protection is determined as 40 per cent of the distance between the prices of two consecutive scale-up purchases. The number of shares for which the stop-loss order is entered is that bought at the previous level, for on a scale-up, purchase commitments are kept separate. Reference is made again to our example of normal-zone operation on a scale-up purchase schedule. The initial purchase unit is 16 shares at 60; the second is 15 shares at 67¼. After the second unit is purchased, a stop-loss order on the original 16 shares is entered at 62⅝ (40 per cent of the distance between 60 and 67¼). If this order is executed during a subsequent decline, then at least some profit is protected, and the 15 shares bought at 67¼ become the start of a new purchase program. If the price continues to rise and a third unit is bought (13 shares at 75⅝), new stop-loss orders are entered on the first and second units. The first is to sell 16 shares at 70½ (40 per cent of the distance between 67¼ and 75⅝), and the previous order to sell at 62⅝ is canceled. The second is to sell 15 shares at 70½, thus protecting profits on both of the first two purchase units.

The New England Plan has not been in operation long enough to provide practical tests of operations in actual markets over a sufficiently long period. Since most of the market action since the plan's inception has been upward, insufficient fluctuation has taken place to really test the plan. However, an actual operation conducted in St. Joseph Lead common stock, with a starting fund of $5000, covering the period December 15, 1949 through January 28, 1953, showed the following results:[6]

	DOLLARS	PER CENT
Amount of fund, 12/15/49	5000.00	
Amount of fund, 1/28/53	6176.54	
a. Cash, 1/28/53	1673.54	
b. Stock (114 shares)	4503.00	
Appreciation		23.5
Total reinvested profits	1424.15	
Total dividends withdrawn	690.50	

A hypothetical test conducted for a longer period in General Motors common stock better reveals the long-term results that are potential in the New England Plan. The price of the stock on January 2, 1937, was 63; it was again 63 on February 5, 1947, having undergone a complete price cycle. If an investor had put $4000 into the stock at the beginning of the period and had held throughout, his account would have shown no capital gain at all. But if he had managed his account according to the New England Plan, his original fund would have grown to $8403 by the end of the price cycle.

[6] This actual test of the New England Plan is explained more fully in reference 17.

The hypothetical test assumed that dividends were withdrawn periodically as received but that capital gains were reinvested, which would account for some part of the increase in value. Results are summarized as follows:[7]

	DOLLARS	PER CENT
Amount of fund, 1/2/37	4000.00	
Amount of fund, 2/5/47	8403.00	
a. Cash, 2/5/47	4308.00	
b. Stock (65 shares)	4095.00	
Appreciation		110
Total reinvested profits	2738.60	
Total dividends withdrawn	1589.75	
Average annual return		10.73

It should be observed that the period selected for this hypothetical test was a very good one, since it was characterized by fairly wide price swings in most stocks and particularly in General Motors. Whether it could be considered typical of results obtainable under all conditions is problematical. At any rate it may be considered probable that, given a long enough period and a reasonable degree of fluctuation in a stock more or less in conformity with its past price history, an annual average return of approximately 7 or 8 per cent could be considered a reasonable possibility. Such return includes both dividends received and capital gains, it being customary under this plan, as under the others designed for individual investors, to withdraw capital gains and thus augment current income.

EVALUATION

What can we say of these individual-stock formula plans in critical evaluation? Tests conducted under actual conditions prove that they can produce moderately favorable results over a long enough period. They deal in individual stocks rather than in averages of stocks, and thus should theoretically have available to them

[7] For a more detailed account of this hypothetical test of the New England Plan, see reference 6.

more possibilities of capitalizing on individual fluctuations. More-over, they always provide for some kind of positive market action, no matter which way the price moves. Scale-up purchasing provides for accumulation of a position in a stock, should the price rise rather than fall after the initial commitment. The individual investor is freed from the necessity for constant market observation, since stop-loss protective selling orders, as well as purchase orders, are entered on a good-until-canceled basis. He is also freed from consider-able worry over his market commitments, for if the price rises, he will be able to sell some of his holdings, and if the price falls, he will be able to add to them.

However, endorsement of these individual-stock plans must necessarily be qualified by certain critical observations. In their ef-fort to provide for some positive market action no matter which way the price of a stock may move, it appears that these plans depart more and more from the original formula-plan idea. For example, the Burlingame Plan's provision for selling out at a loss 25 per cent of the shares after a fully invested position in a stock is attained is definitely not in accord with the customarily assumed principles of formula-plan operation. The argument of the sponsor that such ac-tion provides cash to buy still more shares at lower prices would be sound only if the lower prices were reached. There is just as much chance that they will not be reached, that the price movement may reverse itself after sale at a loss had taken place. Thus more or less permanent damage to the principal of the fund could be inflicted. The possibility of frequent whipsawing as well as the ever-present realization that the lower the price of a stock sinks, the more attrac-tive it becomes as a purchase, not a sale, make this feature of the Burlingame Plan seem to the impartial observer one of highly ques-tionable value.

Furthermore, the revised Howe Plan permits the exercise of so much personal judgment that its resemblance to more orthodox for-mula planning seems largely coincidental. Originally it attempted to project the future price range of a stock from detailed observa-tion of past price records. But in the dynamic world of business, the unreliability of this should become immediately apparent. What kind of logic is there to the assumption that, because a stock has shown a certain average degree of price fluctuation in the past, it must continue to do so in the future? Even the Howe Plan sponsors are alert to this difficulty and are trying to overcome it by their newly adopted revisions. But an attempt to change the long-term trend line every time some new factor develops or every time the cost of living changes by a certain amount would leave the investor in an almost continual state of perplexity. Moreover, how is one to judge whether the effect of a change in a value determinant will be a permanent or a temporary one? There might be some justification for changing the trend extrapolation if the effect were permanent; but consider the difficulty involved later on in placing intelligent price orders if the effect were temporary and if the trend line had already been changed to adjust to it. Then too, the danger of using convertible bonds as a medium of investment for the primary or defensive reserve seems to be one of which the sponsors are either totally or only dimly aware. In strict formula-plan operation, there must be no thought of speculative gain on defensive securities; their primary attribute should be stability of price. Because convertible bonds, by their very nature, are susceptible to a considerable degree of price instability, it appears that a plan that uses them as defensive securities subjects the investor to needless and inordinate risks.

Both the Burlingame and the New England plans also permit scale-up purchasing as an integral feature of operation. This too runs counter to one of the principles upon which formula plans were originally based: purchasing only on a scale-down after the trend line has been crossed. Purchases are never permitted above the trend line by the usual variable-ratio plan. Perhaps the reasoning behind the scale-up–purchase feature of the individual-stock plans is that, because they do not give primary importance to a trend line in their operation, they have less facility for determining when a stock is overvalued and when it is undervalued. Thus if the initial commitment were made when the price was low, a subsequent rise in the price would leave the account sold out with no further chance of getting back in. That is why these plans operate differently in a rising market than in a falling market. In the former, as the price rises and as new scale-up purchases are made, each successive commitment is treated as a separate lot and profit-protecting stop-loss orders are placed on the lots purchased at lower prices. Thus these plans offer the possibility of some definite action by the investor—regardless of the direction of the price move—and perhaps some additional flexibility is thereby achieved.

In its favor it may be said that the scale-up–purchase feature could not involve the fund in a fully invested position at market peaks and thus expose it to considerable shrinkage in market value in a subsequent decline. Since each purchase is treated as a separate lot, any price decline would be likely to cause execution of the stop-loss orders centered on the previously purchased lots. By this means, some profit would be retained, and the last lot purchased would provide the basis for a new stock-purchase program on the downside.

It has been indicated that the New England Plan attempts to divide a stock's projected price range into three zones: normal, above normal, and below normal. The plan also employs a trend line—a 10-year moving average of past prices. Given these tools, the plan should support some evaluation of the current price of a stock: whether it is over- or undervalued. Yet scale-up purchasing is still permitted. It seems that the individual-stock plans try to do too much for the investor and, in doing so, may expose him to needless risk.

The author also feels that the manner of setting stop-loss order prices as a profit-protecting measure deserves some appraisal. Both the Burlingame and New England plans include the use of stop-loss orders. The former proposes to enter them on the basis of some sort of average of intermediate price fluctuations in the past. To apply such an average to the future—to suppose, in other words, that a past average would be typical of future secondary reactions—would seem to be the height of optimism. Probably no fluctuation in the future will exactly duplicate any one in the past, much less an average of past movements. If the criterion of an average is strictly applied, it would appear that the maximum profit potentialities from stop-loss orders would not be capable of realization. If it is not strictly applied, then reliance must be placed almost entirely on personal judgment, which may be considered equivalent to guesswork.

The New England Plan, we have seen, is much more rigid and inflexible in the way it sets its stop-loss prices. A different procedure is used for a declining market than for a rising one, as was previously indicated. Yet how can one be sure that the fixed percentages will tend to maximize profit? The answer seems to be: one can not. Of course, the sponsors may be able to demonstrate that, given a sufficient degree of price fluctuation to execute the stop-loss orders, some profit would accrue. But they invariably fail to provide a comparison between the profit that accrued according to the plan and the maximum profit that might have been possible as a result of the actual price fluctuation. It appears to the author that emphasis upon fixed percentages, when they are applied to a definitely "unfixed" future, seems to be unrealistic and to detract considerably from maximum gain that might have been obtained from the actual price movement. The same argument of excessive rigidity seems equally applicable to the primary reliance of these plans on historical price records of individual stocks as indications of the future price pattern.

The objection may also be raised that individual-stock plans, if followed strictly, would be too complicated for the average individual. They presuppose considerable research into historical price movements, which the average investor may be unwilling to undertake. The mathematical computations, moreover, may be too involved for the individual to comprehend thoroughly or to follow through regularly. An obvious answer to this line of criticism would be that the investor could delegate the problems of computation and selection to the professional sponsors, who would undertake to advise him periodically. But this would involve investment-counsel fees, which would have the effect of reducing the net average annual return to the investor.

In addition, all of these plans suggest the use of a minimum fund for each stock in which operations are conducted. This minimum is usually $4000 or $5000. But this is only for one stock. In order to obtain adequate diversification, an investor should perhaps simultaneously commit himself to five or six different stocks. Thus, to maximize his benefits from an individual-stock plan, the investor should be prepared to commit a minimum of $20,000 or $25,000 to his program. This capital requirement alone may be sufficient to eliminate a good many investors who otherwise might be interested.

Finally, it should be pointed out in critical appraisal that the use of individual-stock plans considerably narrows the field of security selection. Under a more conventional formula plan, which adjusts the proportions between defensive and aggressive securities on the basis of the movements of some well-recognized market average, stock selection is more flexible. The formula plan merely establishes the time at which transfers shall take place. The actual selection of stocks to be bought or sold at the transfer points is within the discretion of the formula-plan manager. An opportunity might thus be available to improve the quality of issues held in the fund by eliminating weaker ones—those that do not seem to justify retention from a profit standpoint—and by holding on to, or even adding to, the stronger ones—those that seem to offer greater profit potential. The individual-stock plans, however, apply a separate formula to each stock and, as time goes on, the investor might find himself disposing of the stronger issues and retaining the weaker ones. In the long run, this practice might conceivably fail to conform to his own best interests and objectives.

Chapter 7

Dollar Averaging

In previous chapters, we have been primarily concerned with methods of achieving better timing for sizable funds that have already been accumulated. Dollar averaging does not apply to accumulated funds; it is, in fact, a *means* of accumulating a fund. Its basic principles are few and simple, but their application requires diligence, patience, and a rigid personal discipline on the part of the investor. If steadfastly followed, a dollar-averaging program will yield satisfactory and profitable results over a period of time.

Any program of dollar averaging has these two major features:

1. A fixed dollar sum.
2. A regular periodic interval.

In initiating a program of this kind, then, the investor must be prepared to commit, to the purchase of common stocks, a fixed, definite dollar amount at regular, definite periodic intervals. To illustrate, he must be prepared to invest, say, $1000 every three months, or $500 every month, or $2500 every six months. The amount that is decided upon will be determined by the financial resources at the disposal of the individual, and whether it is large or small is immaterial. What is important is that the sum be available for investment at regular time intervals. The investor who follows a program of dollar averaging is thus operating in a manner that is counter to the usual one. Most individuals invest their surplus funds by buying fixed numbers of shares at varying dollar amounts. The dollar-averaging investor, on the other hand, buys varying numbers of shares in fixed dollar amounts.

The basic dollar-averaging principle is this: By investing the same dollar amount at regular time intervals, the investor will acquire more shares when prices are low than when they are high. This will have the effect of keeping average cost down. Furthermore, when prices are high, the fixed dollar sum will be able to purchase fewer shares, and this will tend to reduce the risk of large capital loss;[1] when prices are low, the fixed sum will purchase a greater number of shares, and this will tend to increase the possibility of ultimate gain. In carrying out a systematic purchase program, the fact will emerge that the average cost of acquired shares is always less than the average market price. This is illustrated by the hypothetical example in Table 20. It is assumed that the price of a selected stock will, over a period of time, move through a complete price cycle. It is also assumed that a sum of $1000 is invested every 6 months. Brokerage commissions, taxes, and odd-lot fees are disregarded in order to simplify the analysis.

The data of Table 20 show that, even though some shares may have been acquired at much higher prices, the total fund will begin to yield a profit once the market price advances to approximately 51 on the upside. Moreover, even if the price of a stock should decline steadily right after purchase and never recover to the starting point, the dollar-averaging method would still provide some measure of protection to the investor against permanent loss. Consider the example illustrated in Table 21. In this case, any recovery in market price to the level of $29.60 will recoup for the investor the total amount committed, and any higher price will produce a profit for the fund.

---

[1] If prices subsequently decline, the less shares the fund holds at high prices, the less becomes the potential damage that high-cost purchases can inflict upon the principal of the fund.

TABLE 20. DOLLAR-AVERAGING PLAN

(Hypothetical operation of the plan over a complete price cycle)

PURCHASE ORDER	PRICE OF STOCK	AMOUNT INVESTED	NUMBER OF SHARES	AVERAGE COST	AVERAGE PRICE
1	50	$1000	20	$50.00	50
2	60	1000	16.7	54.50	55
3	70	1000	14.3	58.80	60
4	80	1000	12.5	63.00	65
5	65	1000	15.4	63.30	65
6	55	1000	18.2	61.70	63¼
7	40	1000	25	57.10	60
8	30	1000	33.3	51.50	56¼
9	45	1000	22.2	50.70	55
10	50	1000	20	50.60	54¼

TOTAL			AVERAGE		
Amount invested		$10,000	Cost per share		$50.60
Number of shares		197	Average price		$54.50

TABLE 21. DOLLAR-AVERAGING PLAN

(Comparison of average cost with average price in a price decline)

PURCHASE ORDER	PRICE OF STOCK	AMOUNT INVESTED	NUMBER OF SHARES	AVERAGE COST	AVERAGE PRICE
1	50	$1000	20	$50.00	50
2	40	1000	25	44.50	45
3	25	1000	40	35.40	38
4	20	1000	50	29.60	34

TOTAL			AVERAGE		
Amount invested		$4000	Cost per share		$29.60
Number of shares		135	Average price		$34.00

The greatest benefits of any dollar-averaging program will accrue when the stocks selected for purchase exhibit regularity of amplitude and of periodicity in their price fluctuations. The greater the degree of volatility, the better the situation for dollar averaging, for not only is average cost reduced as larger numbers of shares are bought at lower prices, but also the prospect for profit is increased by the ability of the stock to recover in price fairly quickly after a previous decline. Of course, it must be expected that, in the execution of any dollar-averaging program, there will be times when the liquidating value of the shares purchased will be below average cost. But this should not prove disturbing to the investor if he is firm in his resolve to continue the program. Dollar averaging must be thought of, essentially, as a long-term method of accumulating stocks. "Long-term" is intended to imply a period of at least 10 years and perhaps not more than 15 or 20 years. In a 10-to-15–year program, it is presumed that sufficient fluctuation will have taken place to produce a relatively low average cost; in other words, the price of the stock or stocks may have undergone one or more complete price cycles. On the other hand, it would probably not be wise to continue a dollar-averaging program indefinitely. (17) It has been suggested above that such a program probably should be followed not longer than 15 or 20 years. The reason for this lies in the fact that, as the fund becomes steadily larger with each successive purchase, the later commitments will have less and less proportional effect on average cost than had the earlier ones. This effect, moreover, will be magnified if a policy of reinvesting current dividends is pursued along with the regular, fixed periodic purchase. The fund conceivably might grow so large that the dividend income would exceed the amount with which the program was initiated.

If the best potential results are promised by a program lasting 10 to 15 years, the investor may well inquire what to do then. It is suggested that he give consideration to winding up the original program and starting a new one. Thus, at the end of 10 years or so, he might compute his average cost; establish a selling level above average cost, say 25 or 35 per cent, at which he would be content to conclude the program; and then enter an open order to sell out the acquired shares during the next price rise in the stock. If he did not wish to sell out, but preferred to keep his funds more or less continually invested, he might convert his dollar-averaging fund into one of the other formula plans discussed in earlier chapters. This would presume, of course, that the fund would be large enough and that the diversification would be adequate enough to warrant the intelligent application of regular formula-plan principles. Thus, in the end, the investor might wind up with two separate programs: (1) a formula-plan fund and (2) a new dollar-averaging fund to which current income surpluses would be periodically committed.

To summarize this line of analysis, we may conclude that while it does not make so much difference when one starts a dollar-averaging program, it *does* make a great difference when one stops. If one should stop when average cost is above liquidating value, liquidation of the account would result in a loss. Average cost would most likely be above liquidating value only in periods of deep economic depression and then perhaps only temporarily; ironically, it is at such times that the investor would probably be laboring under the greatest pressures against continuance. But assuming the program can somehow or other be continued without interruption over the difficult periods, and assuming that the stocks in the fund undergo the usual range of price fluctuation, dollar averaging will always yield satisfactory results.[2]

But certain aspects of a dollar-averaging program are pitfalls for the unwary investor. One of these is the problem of security selection. It must be presumed that the investor has sufficient acumen to pick securities that do not ultimately become worthless or that may be in long-term downtrends, with no worthwhile recoveries in between. Obviously, if a program is started by buying a stock that continues to decline in price until it finally becomes valueless, the whole idea is defeated. One must insist, therefore, that two things be true of a particular stock, if a dollar-averaging program is to be successful: (1) that the company will continue in business as a going concern no matter what economic conditions the future may hold in store and (2) that the price of the stock be more or less subject to cyclical fluctuation.

Another difficulty is the problem of diversification. Good selection combined with adequate diversification will, in time, generally yield good results. But the investor should be alert to any deteriorating situations, and he should eliminate them from the fund as

---

[2] The elements of forecasting implicit in a dollar-averaging program and the relationship of the program to the long-term trend will be discussed in Chapter 8.

soon as they are detected. It would be foolish to continue pouring good money into a situation that was becoming steadily worse, just for the sake of not breaking faith with the dollar-averaging principle. Herein enters the wisdom of as much diversification as the fund will allow.

While the small investor will normally limit himself to one security when he buys, this is not a necessary condition. The possibility is that he might thereby neglect many favorable opportunities for attractive switches as time goes on, and that the security he has selected might turn out to lack the degree of fluctuation he anticipated. The problem of diversification, however, is more illusory than real and does not in any event negate the basic dollar-averaging principle. If the investor wants greater diversification, he can easily apply dollar-averaging to the purchase of closed-end investment-trust shares, or to shares of an open-end mutual fund. Surely there are enough such funds to choose from to satisfy the most conservative or the most speculative urge. Furthermore, if the investor should prefer to buy one stock year in and year out, much of the argument about over-concentration and undue risk would be overcome if he restricted himself to a blue-chip stock. If he preferred a little diversification, he might divide his regular purchase, more or less equally, among several blue-chip favorites, assuming of course that the periodic amount would be large enough to justify the spread.

A third problem is concerned with the continuing periodic availability of funds to carry out the purchase program. Unless the same amount is committed at regular intervals over a period of years, much of the effectiveness of a dollar-averaging program is lost. In advance of his commitment, the investor should be as sure as possible that he can make his periodic investment during good years and bad. If he attempts to adjust the amount to changes in his income or other financial resources, he will probably find himself committing larger sums when prices are high and smaller sums, or perhaps nothing at all, when prices are low. The consequence would be an inordinately high average cost that would seriously impair the profit potential that can normally be anticipated from a soundly conducted dollar-averaging program. With a little advance planning, however, the investor can avoid this development. The amount he selects for periodic investment should be determined largely by three considerations: (1) the regularity of his income flow, (2) the constancy of his living costs, and (3) the availability of savings and other forms of accumulated capital. If the first two factors have any tendency to vary in significant degree, the investor can estimate the average amount that will be available from annual income over a period of years, with deficiencies in years of low income to be made up from savings accumulated in years of relatively high income.

Although the problem of continuous availability of investment funds may bulk large in the individual investor's considerations, it normally presents no trouble at all to the institutional fund. Such institutions as fire, casualty, and life insurance companies, pension funds, open-end mutual funds, and trusts of various kinds, have a steady stream of funds flowing in each year, or perhaps more accurately, each month of the year. Dollar-averaging is made to order for such funds, and periodic purchases can be carried out with an almost definite certainty of their continuance.

MONTHLY INVESTMENT PLAN OF MEMBERS OF THE NEW YORK STOCK EXCHANGE

In early 1954, members of the New York Stock Exchange launched, after considerable study and research, a plan designed to stimulate continuing public interest in acquiring shares of our leading corporations whose common and preferred stocks are listed on the exchange.[3] The plan, if widely accepted, should not only have great publicity value for the exchange itself but it should also benefit the member-brokers. If public interest is broadened and if the

---

[3] Details of this plan are derived from a brochure issued January 1, 1954 by the New York Stock Exchange to publicize the plan upon its introduction. The brochure is entitled *Monthly Investment Plan* and illustrates the salient features by means of certain hypothetical questions and answers.

public is made more conscious of investment possibilities, new forms of savings may be tapped and the volume of business generally increased. The ultimate benefits to member firms also are not to be minimized, for a small investor now may become a large investor later on and thus many potentially profitable accounts may be acquired. The basic principles of the Monthly Investment Plan tie in so closely with dollar averaging that a discussion of the plan is pertinent at this point. The salient features of the plan are these:

1. An individual may invest any amount from $40 to $1000 in any one stock over any period from 1 to 5 years.

2. The selected amount may be invested either monthly or quarterly.

3. Any stock or stocks listed on the New York Stock Exchange may be selected by the investor himself or he may, if he desires, solicit the advice of his broker without charge.

4. The whole dollar amount that the investor agrees to commit periodically is invested upon receipt by the broker, and the exact number of shares, together with fractions of a share calculated to four decimal places, is credited to the individual's account. For example, $50 will purchase 2.6206 shares of a stock selling for $18, and this includes brokerage commission, tax, and odd-lot differential involved in the transaction. (According to the present odd-lot dealer rules the odd-lot differential is now 12½ cents per share on stocks priced under 40 and 25 cents per share on stocks priced at 40 or higher. For a stock selling at 50, the odd-lot purchase price would be 50¼ and the odd-lot sale price would be 49¾.)

5. Any shares purchased under this plan may be delivered to the owner under either of two options: (a) whenever the total number of shares reaches 50 or more or (b) whenever the plan is completed. Delivery of the stock does not normally involve a charge, but if the investor wants his shares delivered in smaller amounts and at more frequent intervals, he is charged $1 plus mailing costs for each separate delivery.

6. The dividends accruing periodically on the shares already purchased may, at the option of the owner, either be mailed to

him by check from the broker or invested in more shares of the stock being purchased.

7. The broker who handles the account reserves the right to terminate it if the investor fails to live up to his agreement. Action toward termination probably would be taken if five or more successive purchases were skipped.

8. The investor may decide to withdraw at any time, in which event the broker will register in the owner's name, on the books of the company, the full number of shares standing to the investor's credit. Any fractional amounts will be sold for cash, and a check covering the proceeds will be sent to the investor.

9. The investor may exercise his privilege of voting full shares in his account at stockholders' meetings by written instruction to his broker.

10. Diversification may be achieved by buying a different stock each month of any quarter. Thus, three different stocks could be accumulated on four separate occasions each year: Stock A in January, April, July, and October; Stock B in February, May, August, and November; and Stock C in March, June, September, and December.

11. The pro rata share of the investor in any stock dividends or stock split-ups declared on the stocks in his account are automatically credited to his account.

12. The pro rata share of the investor in any *rights* (privileged subscriptions) or any *special distributions* are sold and the investor may at his option either receive the proceeds by check or elect that such proceeds be reinvested in additional shares.

As President of the New York Stock Exchange, Mr. Keith Funston, in early 1956, issued a report on the progress of the Monthly Investment Plan.[4] He stated that the number of plans in effect at the end of the second full year of operation had grown to 38,200

---

[4] See *Wall Street Journal*, February 7, 1956.

and represented a total investment of approximately $28,700,000 spread over 737,000 shares. From January 1, 1955, Monthly Investment Plan had been increasing in public acceptance at the rate of over 100 new plans daily. Mr. Funston stated, in addition, that if all the plans then in force were carried through to completion, the total investment would approach $100,000,000.

It also appears that MIP investors are increasingly inclined to put their periodic dividend income into additional shares. At the time of Mr. Funston's report, the percentage of such investors had increased to 82.1 from 78.6 at the start of 1955. The preference of investors leans strongly toward stock issues of the blue-chip variety. At the time of the report, General Electric common stock was the issue most in favor, closely followed by Radio Corporation of America. General Motors was third, and others, in order of relative importance, were Dow Chemical, American Telephone & Telegraph, and Standard Oil of New Jersey.

The report also revealed that MIP investors showed a surprising interest in stocks in the medium- to higher-priced range. Such high-priced issues as duPont and International Business Machines were two common stocks—both in the price range above $200 per share—that were favored by only 873 individual plans. However, the most popular issues were those in the $50 to $60 price range. On an industry basis, the order of preference was chemicals, utilities, electrical equipment, petroleum, natural gas, and automobiles.

The average number of plans started daily during the 2-year period was 116, and the total number of plans started during the same period was 58,200. Of the 20,000 plans discontinued by January 25, 1956, most had been either written on a 1-year basis or dropped in favor of regular brokerage accounts. Of the total number of plans started, 55 per cent showed a preference for purchase on a monthly rather than a quarterly basis.

The Monthly Investment Plan agreement between broker and investor is shown in Figure 4, parts 1–4.

M. I. P. 2 R 12-53

MONTHLY INVESTMENT PLAN

P. O. BOX 209   NEW YORK 5, N. Y.

PURCHASE ORDER

ORIGINAL
Send To Odd Lot Dealer

_____, 195___

Gentlemen:

IT IS MY PRESENT INTENTION TO INVEST $ _____

_____
(Name of Stock)

monthly
quarterly IN

COMMENCING ON THE DATE MY FIRST REMITTANCE IS CREDITED TO MY ACCOUNT AND

TERMINATING _____, 19____ ON THE NEW YORK STOCK EXCHANGE,

Each remittance for my account, less your commission, will be applied by you, as my broker, to the purchase of full shares of the stock and/or a fractional interest in a share. Purchases will be made at the first odd-lot price established after the day the remittance is credited to my account.

I reserve the right to cancel this order at any time, without penalty or charge, by written notice to you. You also may cancel this order at any time by written notice to me at the address below. Purchases made before receipt of a cancellation notice will not be affected by such notice.

FIGURE 4, part 1

Cash dividends, and proceeds of sales of rights and of special distributions, received for my account, are to be paid to me ☐, or reinvested ☐. (Check one)

A certificate in my name for all the full shares in this account should be mailed to me promptly after the termination date of this order ☐, or when the number of shares amounts to 50 or more ☐. (Check one).

THE TERMS AND CONDITIONS SET FORTH ON THE REVERSE SIDE ARE PART OF THIS PURCHASE ORDER,

_____
(Signature of Customer)

_____
(City and State)

┌─────────────────────────────────┐
│   │
│ DO NOT WRITE IN THIS SPACE   │
│   │
└─────────────────────────────────┘

_____
(Name of Member Firm)

MR.
MRS.
MISS _____
(Name of Customer - Please Print)

_____
(Street Number)

_____
(Member Firm's Identifying Number - Not to Exceed 4 Digits)

_____
(Initials of Partner or Officer Authorizing Opening of Account)

FIGURE 4, part 2

TERMS AND CONDITIONS

The following terms and conditions shall govern transactions under this purchase order and the voting and handling of securities and the conduct of my account under this order by you and your successors.

1. All provisions of the Constitution, rules and regulations, and all customs and usages, of the New York Stock Exchange, as from time to time in effect, shall apply.

2. Your commission will be at the minimum rates from time to time in effect on the New York Stock Exchange on purchases involving $100 or more, and at 6% if the purchase involves less than $100.

3. You may use the services of one or more other member firms of the New York Stock Exchange (who may be the dealers from whom purchases are made under this order), as your agent to make and receive payments and deliveries and combine this and other similar orders of other member firms and of your and their customers. You are authorized on my behalf to enter into a written custody agreement with any firm so acting as your agent, providing, among other things, that such shares (including shares in which I have a fractional interest) are to be held or disposed of by such custodian for me and subject at all times to my order. Shares and fractional interests so held may be registered in the name of the custodian or its nominee and may be combined with shares held for you and other member firms and your and their customers. Any member firm acting for you in one or more of such capacities may act on instructions given by you for my account and, except as otherwise provided in any such custody agreement, such firm shall be responsible only to you.

FIGURE 4, part 3

148

4. My pro-rata share of stock dividends received in shares of the stock being purchased and my pro-rata share of all stock split-ups are to be credited to my account. Other distributions of securities and rights to subscribe are to be sold and my pro-rata share of the proceeds are to be invested or paid to me as directed on the face of this order.

5. A change in the security (except one resulting from a stock split-up) which results in the cancellation of orders in the hands of odd-lot dealers and specialists, shall suspend this order until receipt of further instructions from me. Other changes in the security shall not suspend this order.

6. Upon the cancellation, or upon the specified termination date of this order, or the cancellation of unfilled purchases under it, a certificate in my name for the number of full shares held for me will be mailed to me, any fractional interest in my account will be sold and a check for the cash proceeds of such sale and a final statement of my account will be sent to me.

7. At any time I may, without cancelling this order, direct that a certificate for any number of full shares held for my account be mailed to me. For any such special advance delivery of less than 50 shares a service charge of $1 plus any shipping expenses will be paid by me.

8. On receipt by you of advice of my death or legal incapacity, this order will be terminated as to future purchases and any securities and cash shall be held pending receipt of proper authorizations and instructions.

Courtesy of Members of the New York Stock Exchange, 1956
New York, N.Y.

FIGURE 4, part 4

149

Chapter 8

The Pitfalls

When they are formally presented by their individual sponsors, formula plans look very attractive on paper but the question of real interest to the investor—whether an individual or an institution—is the degree to which they can stand the test of practical application. In this connection, hindsight is not always a reliable guide. A plan may have worked very well during selected periods in the past. Indeed, the periods for testing may have been chosen because they corresponded rather closely with expected theoretical results, because the conditions, in other words, were those in which the mechanics of the particular plan might work most satisfactorily. If that is the case, one can reasonably expect the plan to work as well in the future only if such conditions again prevail. But who today can say with assurance what conditions will prevail in the securities markets in coming years, what factors will govern the movements of prices, and whether history can or will repeat itself?

It is, then, important that we critically examine the fundamental nature of formula plans and try to develop a basis of evaluation in the interest of complete investor preparedness. To this point, our objective has been to find out why and how formula plans came into original acceptance, to point out some fundamental presumptions upon which all such plans are based, and to describe the manner in which the two broad categories operate. It is the purpose of this chapter to examine the other side of the argument, to inquire into the limitations and disadvantages, the potential shortcomings and pitfalls of formula plans. This will involve appraisal of the validity of fundamental presumptions, of the degree to which forecasting is or is not eliminated, and of the difficulties inherent in certain methods of determining trend lines that are intended to be guides to the future. But first, let us begin this evaluation with a look at some general considerations.

CRITICAL OBSERVATIONS

RIGIDITY IN A CHANGING WORLD

One of the primary features of formula plans is the attempt to find a substitute for judgment in the timing of security purchases and sales. Particularly in the operation of variable-ratio plans, certain preestablished rules are intended to guide the investor in making all transfers from stocks to bonds or from bonds to stocks. If the investor has confidence in his plan, he should not let judgment interfere with its operation. In fact, the elimination of judgment is hailed as a cardinal virtue because it restrains the investor from succumbing to his emotions and being carried along with the crowd, and thus from making decisions that are possibly hasty and unwise. No doubt there are times when the freedom from emotionalism would be an advantage, but it can be pointed out with equal confidence that there are times when the application of judgment and common sense would be wiser than adherence to a rigidly preconceived plan.

Most formula plans, by their very nature, prescribe fixed rules of operation to govern a situation that, by its very nature, is dynamic. Professor J. Fred Weston comments significantly on this feature when he says:

Formula plans are weak in that they represent an inflexible judgment to be applied mechanically to changing circumstances. The weakness of a fixed plan of action in a changing universe is indeed a limitation.[1]

[1] "Some Theoretical Aspects of Formula Timing" in *Journal of Business,* copyright 1949 by the University of Chicago. (38)

A variable-ratio plan is generally constructed on a historical basis; the upper and lower limits between which the stock market is likely to fluctuate in the future are merely the projection of past trends. If the projection, which is supposed to represent normal or long-range value, is based on a moving-average or on an arithmetic or geometric plot of a trend, it is a reflection of the past; the selection of intervals between stock-and-bond transfer points is generally determined by the intervals that have proved satisfactory in the past.

But the investor has no assurance that the pattern of projection, no matter how well based on the past, will prove applicable to the future. And once such rigidities are incorporated into a plan, they automatically become the basis for action by the investor; if the future pattern of security-price fluctuation fails to conform to the plan's projection, unfavorable results will undoubtedly follow. The plan may call for either the disposal of securities too early in a rise or their acquisition too early in a decline, and the investor might subsequently be faced with long periods of immobility, having been frozen into a position while security prices are still moving against him. The formula-plan investor must be on his guard against such an eventuality; it is neither invariable nor inevitable, but it is certainly possible. *If* security-price fluctuations stay within the projected range, well and good; if they move out of the range for extended periods, the investor must give some thought to reappraisal of his plan. Perhaps some of the practical difficulty involved in the potential divergence of the actual price movement from the projected one might be overcome by periodic re-examination of the plan and by incorporating revisions to bring the plan's operation into better conformity with reality. It is better, perhaps, to allow *some* human judgment to enter than to stay out of harmony with reality for extended periods; to do so would considerably alleviate the dangers and risks of continued inflexibility. And this need not necessarily mean complete abandonment of all formula principles; their application should merely be modified under certain conditions.

THE PROBLEM OF INVESTOR COMPLIANCE

At times during the operation of a formula plan, the investor may become impatient with the results and may be strongly tempted to abandon it entirely. This might be true if the investor found that his plan involved him in extended periods of inactivity. Perhaps he sold out too soon and common-stock prices are still rising; or perhaps he bought too soon and prices are still falling. It would require personal courage of a very high order to continue to adhere to the plan. But even if his plan were working reasonably well, public emotionalism might be running so rampant that the investor would find it difficult, if not impossible, to oppose the current psychology. He might feel that by disregarding what his plan required at the moment and by gearing his operations temporarily to the prevailing trend, he would be able to increase his profits. But he might thereby be falling victim to the very errors his plan was designed to avoid.

THE PROBLEM OF UNIVERSAL ADOPTION

If the same formula plan were to be adopted for the management of all the large institutional funds in the United States, the problem of security transfers might become insuperable: all the funds would be bought and sold at the same time, and the action that the formula plan was designed to achieve might well be completely defeated. Such large shifts of invested capital would be involved that all formula plans might become ineffectual. Conceivably the price movement occasioned by large simultaneous transfers might never go beyond the first transfer point from stocks to bonds on the upside and the first such point from bonds to stocks on the downside. Such action would of course severely mitigate the potentially desirable results of formula-plan operation. While the possibility is not of any immediate practical importance, it might conceivably create some kind of problem for insurance companies, investment trusts, mutual funds, and large estates, if formula-plan operation ever sees a more widespread adoption. The problem is mentioned here solely to indicate a possible source of difficulty. At the present time, there is very little likelihood that anything along this line will develop, because there is substantial diversity of institutional plans now in operation and also because there are basic structural and operational differences between the plans.

A collateral problem may present itself to the small investor who has a fund of limited size at his disposal. The problem he must face is the inability to commit a sufficiently large fund to aggressive securities to achieve adequate diversification. To achieve best results under a formula plan, the stock portion of the fund must be representative of the general market, and the individual stocks should fluctuate in price rather closely with the market index on which the plan is based. This can only be achieved through proper diversification: the less the degree of diversification, the greater the inherent risk. Therefore, the small investor either should not resort to any formula-plan commitment or should confine his stock purchases to the securities of mutual funds and investment trusts which would at least provide him with some indirect diversification. This, however, might well be at the expense of ultimate capital gain, due to the fact that fluctuation in the prices of mutual-fund shares is more limited than that of the common stocks that comprise mutual-fund portfolios.

The Problem of Security Selection

In Chapter 2, certain general presumptions upon which the formula-plan idea is based were pointed out. One of these concerned the nature of price fluctuation in the aggressive portion of the fund. It was presumed that the investor, under formula operation, would be able to select securities for the stock fund that would experience price movements more or less in close correspondence with the fluctuation of some market index, presumably the DJIA, around which the buying-and-selling action of the plan might be constructed. For best results from a capital-gain stand-point, fluctuation would have to be similar both in timing and amplitude. But what if the DJIA failed to be representative of the general market for common stocks listed on the New York Stock Exchange? The DJIA is composed of only 30 leading industrial stocks of the blue-chip variety. Yet there are approximately 1500 different issues listed on that exchange. Is it not conceivable that the DJIA might one day move upward while the rest of the general list remained unchanged, or that the DJIA might stand still while the rest of the list moved downward? The amount and frequency of transfer between the aggressive and defensive portions of the fund would be geared to the movements of the DJIA; yet if a transfer point were reached calling, for example, for the sale of some stocks that might have declined in the meantime, serious damage to the corpus of the fund would be inflicted.

Of course, it was pointed out in Chapter 2 that a formula plan is essentially a timing, and not a selection, device. The investor has the problem of proper security selection no matter what system or method he chooses to use for timing his purchases and sales. Re-emphasis of the point serves to alert the investor to the crucial importance of ensuring as closely a parallel movement as possible between the individual stocks comprising the aggressive fund and the DJIA. A small mistake here might easily jeopardize much of the potential advantage otherwise available under good formula-plan operation.

A problem related to that of security selection concerns the composition of the defensive fund. All formula plans assume that the securities that comprise the defensive portion will be relatively immune to price fluctuation.[2] The defensive fund is designed to be the temporary repository of the capital gains that accrue periodically from the sale of aggressive-fund securities. For maximum gain the defensive fund should remain intact until it is again drawn upon to provide the purchasing power for reaccumulation of ag-

---

[2] Of course, if the defensive fund consisted solely of cash or a savings account, the problem of price fluctuation would be eliminated.

gressive securities during a price decline. Statistical comparisons of results achieved under different types of formula plans usually direct attention to capital gains from the sale of aggressive securities and tacitly assume that the defensive securities have not changed in price. This may suit the purpose of statistical comparison, but the well-informed investor knows from practical experience that bond prices also fluctuate over time. The fluctuation may be attributed chiefly to two factors.

1. Movement of interest rates as conditions in the money market become alternately easy or tight and as the influence of Federal Reserve monetary policy on credit expansion or contraction manifests itself.[3]

2. The possible deterioration in credit rating of a bond due to unfavorable economic developments affecting the company in question.

Is it not then possible that, over a period of time, the gains realized from timely disposal of stocks may be partially offset by losses sustained among the defensive securities? Any such losses would generally tend to be proportional to the degree of fluctuation in interest rates; the more adverse the movement in the latter, the greater the potential loss. However, this is a sort of two-edged sword. While losses in defensive securities may be sustained due to an unfavorable movement in interest rates, the reverse is also true —gains may accrue because of a favorable movement in such rates. A good deal depends on when the formula plan was initiated and on the level of interest rates then prevailing. A good deal also depends on the alertness of the investor to the degree of change occurring and on his ability to protect himself from the worst effects of such change. Some protection could be achieved by a constant review of the defensive securities and by taking action such as the conversion of long-term bonds into shorter-term obligations, as well as by the prompt replacement of a deteriorating issuer's

[3] Bond prices tend to maintain an inverse relationship to interest rates. Thus as interest rates advance, bond prices tend to decline, and vice versa.

debt obligation with one of a company not subject to an unfavorable economic prospect.

ELIMINATION OF MARKET FORECASTS

One of the great advantages claimed for formula plans is that they do not require the investor to make periodic forecasts of the future course of stock prices. They do not, it is said, require any judgment on his part concerning the matter of timing. This is a distinct advantage, it is claimed, because the investor, having the "when" problem more or less mechanically solved for him by his formula, can devote more serious attention to the problem of security selection. It seems worthwhile at this point to inquire into the validity of the claim.

The ardent formula-plan supporter would probably deny that any element of forecasting was involved in dollar-averaging or the equalization plans (constant-dollar and constant-ratio). He might be induced to admit that some judgment must necessarily enter into the construction of a variable-ratio plan, for here a clear projection of the future is required. However, he would be likely to say to this: "I admit a projection is necessary, but my forecast is of a long-term variety. I am not forecasting the near-term or cyclical course of prices. And it is from the cyclical movements that I expect my formula will return to me the greatest gain."

But let us look at this more closely and try to determine more accurately the extent to which forecasting enters into the operation of different types of formula plans. Weston (38) claims that forecasting is inherent in every type of formula plan. Even dollar-averaging, he points out, contains the implicit forecasts that (1) security prices will continue to fluctuate, (2) the amplitude of cyclical movements of prices will be fairly regular, and (3) the long-term price trends of securities bought under such a program will not be unfavorable. He goes on to say:

Dollar averaging assumes for its success that a cyclical pattern of price fluctuation is forecast wherein the area under the positive alternation is not substantially greater than the area under the negative alternation.

He concludes his estimate of dollar-averaging with this statement:

The success of the simplest type of formula plan, dollar averaging, depends upon a favorable secular trend and a not too unfavorable cyclical pattern. There is implicit forecasting, therefore, in the prototype of formula plans.[4]

It may be axiomatic to state that the degree of forecasting inherent in formula plans is directly proportional to the amount of risk assumed and that the amount of risk is proportional to the amount of expected capital gain. Thus a greater degree of forecasting would attach itself to variable-ratio plans than to the equalization plans because the former are supposed to be productive of greater gain than the latter under similar conditions of price fluctuation. Constant-ratio plans are content with the realization of a moderate, assured capital gain over a complete market cycle in return for a minimization of risk. But even here the situation is not devoid of judgment, and some element of forecasting is implicit. In appraising constant-ratio plans in a study made several years ago, Cottle and Whitman observed:

Some forecasting is necessarily involved, contrary to general belief, in the establishment of such a plan. Specifically, there is the underlying prediction that, in the course of its fluctuation, the market will not for an extended period of years remain below the price level existing at the time the plan is inaugurated. Because a constant-ratio plan limits the opportunity for capital appreciation, a small error in this prediction may involve a loss requiring many years to overcome. (25)

A considerable degree of discretion must therefore be exercised when a constant-ratio plan is inaugurated. If it is started when security prices are not in a historically high range, and if the amplitude and periodicity of cyclical fluctuation are fairly regular, it should produce reasonably satisfactory results as a timing device. But if it is started either when security prices are historically high or just prior to a violent decline, its lack of productive results might seriously strain the patience of the investor. He would then have

_____
[4] *Op. cit.*, copyright 1949 by the University of Chicago.

to decide for himself whether to commit initially 50 per cent of the fund to stocks or whether to commit some lesser amount, say 30 or 35 per cent. He would also face the decision of how high is high in stock prices. What is historically high today may be historically low 10 years from now. These are questions requiring a rare delicacy of human judgment.

Another important factor in the operation of a constant-ratio plan is the choice of percentages above and below the constant ratio at which transfers will be made to equalize both the aggressive and defensive funds. It would be a very fortunate circumstance, indeed, if the choice of transfer points just happened to correspond closely to the tops and bottoms of cyclical fluctuations of stock prices in the future. On this point, Weston (38) has the following to say:

The greatest gain under the equalizing plan can be achieved by choosing percentages which coincide with the maximum amplitude of each cyclical swing of security prices. But the maximum range is likely to vary from cycle to cycle. The positive and negative alternations are not likely to be symmetrical. Therefore to maximize gain calls for the exercise of considerable forecasting skill.[5]

It has already been mentioned that variable-ratio plans require, in their construction, considerably more forecasting than do either the equalization or dollar-averaging plans. Here certain decisions are crucial to success, and they all involve the uncertain future. What shall be determined as the expected range of stock-price fluctuation in the future? By what method shall the line of normal value be calculated—the trend line around which future price fluctuations should take place in approximately equal amplitude? How much validity attaches to the projection of this line into the future? At what intervals in the movement of the DJIA shall transfer points be established? Should these intervals be based on percentage movement or on number-of-actual-points movement? How great should these intervals be, and how many should there be? How should the buying-and-selling schedule be

[5] *Op. cit.*, copyright 1949 by the University of Chicago.

set up? What should be the maximum percentage that will be represented by stocks and bonds at the tops and bottoms of price movements? How much of the fund should be transferred from stocks to bonds, or vice versa, at each transfer point? Should any delaying action, such as the halfway rule, be employed?

These questions must be faced in the establishment of any variable-ratio plan and the answers cannot be compromised. The answers demand a rare combination of good judgment and forecasting skill. They seem to point to the fact that variable-ratio plans are not, after all, so mechanistic and so automatic as their sponsors would sometimes have us believe.

To observe that forecasting is implicit in varying degree in different kinds of formula plans is not intended in any way to detract from the otherwise substantial advantages that formula plans can offer the investor. Any other timing device would perhaps involve as much if not more forecasting skill, for both short- and long-range predictions would be required. Once the initial problems are solved, however, and once the rules of operation are established, formula-plan operation can become more or less routine and automatic. Successful results will then depend upon the correctness of the long-range forecast that was made. A good estimate can make the investor extremely happy with his plan; a bad estimate will produce the opposite reaction. The advantage of a formula plan to the investor over any alternative timing device lies in a difference in the degree of risk assumed. A formula plan's value is a function of both the gains that may reasonably be expected and the risk to which the investor is exposed; if the gains are greater than those obtainable by any other forecasting method with the same degree of risk, then the appeal and attractiveness of the formula plan to the investor has genuine merit and substance. In this connection, Ezra Solomon observes:

The profit rate is thus, in the main, dependent not on any intrinsic worth of a plan but is related directly to the degree of dependence on a prediction and hence arises out of the act of risk-bearing it carries in the extent to which it backs that prediction. (34)

THE PROBLEM OF THE LONG-TERM TREND

The concept of "long-term trend" as applied to formula plans involves not only the general direction in which stock prices will move but also the relative width of the channel within which they can be expected to fluctuate cyclically. The success of any variable-ratio plan hinges directly upon the degree of correspondence between future price movements and the projection on which the buying-and-selling schedule is based. In fact, it might be said that this is the very sum and substance of variable-ratio or sliding-scale plans. Some degree of awareness of the long-term trend is also important to the investor who operates by a dollar-averaging or constant-ratio plan. But neither of these latter plans is vitally dependent on the long-term trend; all they require is that it not be unfavorable, a point that is discussed in the preceding section. This section is devoted chiefly to the relationship of the long-term trend to the variable-ratio plan.

In the original construction of any variable-ratio plan, most careful consideration must be given to three things:

1. The determination of a trend line, the statistical approximation of the basic, underlying value of stocks. If current stock prices are close to this value line, the stocks may be said to be properly priced for investment purposes.

2. The determination of the extremes above and below the trend line at which stock positions should be at a minimum and maximum, respectively.

3. The number of transfer points between the upper and lower limits, points at which stock holdings are reduced as prices rise and increased as prices fall.

These three basic features are common to all variable-ratio plans. The different means that are employed to implement them in practical operation constitute not only the basic differences between the individual plans themselves but also the reason for their varying claims to success.

Since a trend line is so important to a variable-ratio plan, the method used in its determination becomes all-important. Broadly, there are three methods:

1. Manually fitting or computing a trend projection.
2. Calculating a moving average.
3. Determining intrinsic value.

The first two methods depend upon actual past stock prices, generally as measured by the DJIA, while the third depends upon the past relationship of stock prices to such value determinants as earnings, dividends, and book values.

Trend Projection. Trend projection is a method of determining a trend line by charting the past fluctuations of stock prices, as represented by the DJIA or some other well-recognized market index, and manually fitting a line that approximately divides the cyclical fluctuations into equal parts. However constructed, the trend line describes a level around which stock prices have tended to fluctuate from the time of the earliest data to the present. Graphically, it is a long line sloping upwards to the right on a chart. The outstanding current application of the trend-line-projection method is the Keystone Seven-Step Plan, of which the trend, manually fitted on a geometric-chart scale, exhibits an average annual increase of about 3 per cent. The long-term trend for the future, then, is simply an extension of the trend line on the Keystone chart. Long-term growth has been due to such factors as population growth, rising standards of living, rising national income, and rapid technological advance. To project this growth into the future is to presume not only that the growth-producing factors will continue to be effective but that they will be so at an average annual rate of 3 per cent. Is this assumption tenable? Professor Marshall D. Ketchum, in an article written in 1948 (30), saw fit to doubt that it is; he comments:

The analysis of more recent stock-price fluctuations gives us some cause to question the assumption that the trend will be as strongly upward in the future as it appears to have been over the entire period from 1897–1946. (30)

Of course, Ketchum wrote his article at a time when stock prices were governed by considerable uncertainty in the postwar markets. He was, perhaps, not in a position to foresee the long rise in stock prices that got under way in the summer of 1949 and persisted with but minor interruptions to 1957. But his observation is still pertinent: he is questioning the validity of the assumption that the future trend of stock prices will, as portrayed by the Keystone Seven-Step Plan, continue upward at the same rate as in the past.

Will the future long-term trend of stock prices obligingly conform to the pattern of the trend projection? What if it changes at a rate that is either greater or less than that projected? What would happen if the secular trend leveled out horizontally or even went into a long-term decline? The trend-line-projection method is relatively incapable of prompt adjustment to such a situation. Moreover, how is the investor to recognize when the trend is changing? If he were certain that the long-term trend of the future would be upward at a more rapid or less rapid rate, he might take appropriate steps to recompute or reconstruct his trend line so that it fitted the changed situation more properly. But how is he to distinguish whether a price fluctuation is the beginning of a changed trend or merely an abnormal phase of a larger cyclical pattern? If stock prices permanently depart from the trend line, should he continue to base buying-and-selling action on it? A failure to recognize promptly a changing long-term trend might produce some very unfortunate results. Then, too, how can the investor be sure that his selection of a trend line was correct, when there are no precise statistical standards and no conclusive tests to prove the validity of any trend projection? Cottle and Whitman comment pointedly on this question when they say:

Because a trend-line projection of stock prices is inflexible and independent of actual market prices, it may depart permanently from the market. The projection of the 1897–1925 geometric trend line illustrates this hazard. Although the extent of the danger is difficult to appraise, the fact that permanent departure may occur produces the attendant risk that temporary departures will create such doubt in the investor's mind that he will abandon the trend line. (4)

The Moving Average. The moving-average method has an advantage over the trend-projection method in that it provides a self-adjusting trend line. There is no danger that stock prices will depart permanently from the trend, for the latter is constructed out of the actual data of past price variations. There will be some element of lag in responsiveness of the moving average to the actual price movement, and this will depend on the length of the time period employed in the construction of the average. The longer the period, the less responsive does the average become; the shorter the period, the more responsive. But, by and large, allowing for this time lag, the moving average will follow in the direction of any change in the long-term movement of stock prices.

The implied assumption in the use of the moving average is that a normal value for stock prices can be determined by a simple arithmetic average of actual prices over an immediately preceding time period. This creates a source of confusion for the investor, for, depending on the time period selected, there could be several different figures for normal value in relation to the current data. If the long-term trend were horizontal, and if there were a certain regularity of amplitude and periodicity to stock-price fluctuations, a moving average of the same period as that of the complete cycle would adequately approximate a line of normal value. But all the historical evidence seems to confirm the fact that the very opposite is true—that stock prices fail to exhibit any regularity of period or degree of fluctuation in their cyclical movements.

What, then, is there to do? Possibly all one can say is that it would be preferable in the use of a moving average not to have too much fluctuation in the trend line itself. Too short a time period, say, 3 to 5 years, would permit too much responsiveness in the trend, which would then begin to exhibit minor cycles of its own similar to the fluctuations of the basic data.[6] The longer the period selected for the average, the smoother will be the line, although at the increasing sacrifice of prompt adjustment to significant changes in basic data.

C. Sidney Cottle, in an article published in 1949, has some interesting observations to make in connection with the historical testing of the moving-average method as applied to a hypothetical investment fund operated during the period 1922–1947. (24) For purposes of analysis, he uses a 10-year moving average of the annual means of the DJIA as the trend line and the month-end close of the DJIA to chart actual market action. He establishes a schedule of buying and selling that provides for a 50/50 position at the trend line, with successive reductions in stocks to zero (100 per cent bonds) as prices rise 10, 21, and 33 per cent above the trend line, and successive increases in stocks to 100 per cent (0 per cent bonds) as prices fall 10, 19, and 27 per cent below the trend line. From his study of this hypothetical operation, he draws the following conclusions:

1. During periods of violent market action of marked duration in any single direction, there may be long intervals of inactivity under a formula plan of the type analyzed. Furthermore, these intervals may be of such duration that one might well lose all confidence in the plan.

2. It appears almost inevitable that stocks would be sold out very early under a plan based on a long-term moving average. A ten-year moving average is not sufficiently responsive to the data to take advantage of more than a relatively limited portion of an extended bull market.

3. If a long bull market is followed by an abrupt and drastic decline in stock prices, it also appears inevitable that stocks would be purchased very early. The same lack of responsiveness to current market conditions which resulted in selling stocks too early in the rise, now works to the definite detriment of the fund in a time of rapidly falling prices. (24)

In other words, during periods of violent market action, both up and down, a 10-year moving average would not constitute a reli-

[6] The possibility of being whipsawed frequently by irregular price movements is always present when the period chosen for the moving average is too short.

able trend line. Its usefulness as a timing device would tend to increase in direct proportion to the extent to which actual price
movements reflect greater moderation.

Ketchum also, in the article referred to earlier, is aware of
the problem posed by a changing long-term trend and is concerned
with the development of means to adjust for such a change. (30)
Depending on the direction and the rate at which the long-term
trend changes, a formula plan's zonal limits should also be adjusted. For instance, if the trend is rising at a more rapid rate, the
zonal limits should be adjusted upward correspondingly; if the trend
is becoming more horizontal, the zonal limits should be adjusted
downward correspondingly. Ketchum's problem, then, is to find
some way of establishing the zonal limits so that they will be self-
adjusting no matter what direction the trend takes. In his study he
tries to demonstrate that the use of moving averages provides a
reasonably satisfactory conclusion. What he does is construct a 10-
year moving average of the highs and a 10-year moving average
of the lows of the DJIA for the period 1930–1946. This provides a
broad channel that is itself fluctuating more or less in response to
changes in the trend. Four approximately equidistant trend lines
are then established within this channel to indicate transfer points
between stocks and bonds. In this way, Ketchum claims, the zonal
range would automatically widen or narrow depending upon
whether the amplitude of the actual price fluctuation increases or
decreases.

It appears that Ketchum's refinement of the traditional use of
the moving average suffers from the same limitations that were
discussed above. The zonal range will perhaps be kept flexible and
moving ultimately in the direction of the changing trend, but it
will lag in responsiveness. Again, the longer the period chosen for
the moving average, the greater the lag, and therefore the more
unreliable the results. The moving averages may be indicating a
contraction of the zonal range due to a dampened amplitude of
fluctuation in the past, precisely when the amplitude may be pre-
paring for a much broader expansion. It is likely, too, that the
outer limits of the zonal range will fail to correspond closely with

the actual cyclical peaks and troughs, with a consequent reduction of potential trading gains.

In summary, it is not possible to say that the moving-average method will invariably provide a reliable timing device under all sets of market conditions. Under certain circumstances, it might work reasonably well; under other circumstances, it will not. As long as the long-term trend is subject to change at a variable rate and as long as the periodicity and amplitude of cyclical fluctuation is neither regular nor moderate in extent, moving averages will not prove the complete answer to proper trend line determination. However, this does not necessarily imply that the method must be entirely discarded. Certainly errors will be committed by using a moving average, as they will in any other conceivable method of timing. The important question is: Will the error be less than that arising from alternative methods? As Weston says:

The error incurred by the use of a moving average will be less than the error committed by the use of a significantly erroneous forecast by the use of judgment or any other method. (38)

And again,

The strength of the moving-average method is that it places a limit on the magnitude of the error which might be committed. It thereby minimizes the maximum risk.[7]

The Intrinsic-value Method. The mechanics of constructing a trend line along intrinsic-value concepts are carefully outlined in Chapter 4. It will suffice here to appraise the method more critically and to point up possible limitations and shortcomings.

The intrinsic-value method employs as tools of analysis such basic determinants of common-stock values as earnings per share, dividends per share, book value per share, price-earnings ratios, and disparities of bond and stock yields. From this, it is immediately apparent that trend lines based on the method tend to differ to the extent that different importance is accorded one or more of

[7] *Op. cit.*, copyright 1949 by the University of Chicago.

the factors involved. The following are presumed in the use of the method:

1. That a current value arrived at by the use of the basic value determinants would closely approximate a stock's real, underlying worth, in the light of the most accepted prevailing principles of investment analysis.

2. That past history affords evidence of a constant enough relationship between the basic determinants and stock prices to justify the assumption that the value line has a sound basis of historical support.

An intrinsic-value line, then, is a measure of the fair price of stocks on the basis of current and expectable factors. Any deviation of actual prices above the line indicates some degree of overvaluation, and vice versa. In its favor it must be admitted that this method is flexible in that there could rarely be a permanent departure of actual prices from the trend line. If the assumption of a consistent relationship in the past between stock prices and value-determining factors is accepted, and if there is no reason to suppose that this relationship will change in the future, then the line will always tend to be self-adjusting. Whatever causes the stock prices to change in the future will similarly affect the trend line. Information on such basic factors as earnings, dividends, and book values is now available on a quarterly basis from most of our leading corporations. Thus, the trend is promptly adjustable to changes in the underlying factors and, for this reason, it is the author's opinion that the intrinsic-value line is more responsive to periodic change than is either the moving-average or the trend-line projection method.

What is pertinent about the intrinsic-value method at this point is its reliability as a measure of future value. Chapter 4 presents detailed criticisms of the method with regard to such matters as investor understanding, the mechanics of construction of individual plans, and the relative importance accorded to different factors in different operative plans. The method itself, however, is believed to be based on sound economic relationships, and therefore a trend line so constructed would seem to offer greater promise of reliability with less chance of error than does either the moving-average or the trend-projection method. It thus seems to represent an improvement—a step forward in more adequate trend line determination.

Yet a few words of caution may be in order. The concept of intrinsic value must be thought of as essentially a short-run factor; there would be considerable risk in projecting the value line too far into the future. Since it is based upon currently available data together with the recorded data of the recent past, its validity as a timing device must be construed in terms of the near future rather than the distant future. In addition, its reliability even for the short term depends principally on whether the consistent relationship between stock prices and such factors as earnings and dividends, so observable in the past, will persist into the indefinite future. Nothing on the investment horizon would now indicate that the relationship will *not* be maintained, but if any economic disturbance should alter it in the future, the reliability of the intrinsic-value method would be open to more serious question and reappraisal.

A final criticism concerns the calculation of the arithmetic amount of the intrinsic value itself. Benjamin Graham's Central-value line, it will be recalled, is constructed on the basis of a 10-year moving average of the annual earnings of the composite DJIA and on a capitalization of this average at a rate equivalent to twice the current yield on high-grade bonds. Some difficulties in this method become readily apparent. One concerns the limitations already discussed with respect to the use of any long-term moving average as a reliable indication of a changing trend. Another limitation is the tacit implication that the average-earnings rate reflects a prediction of "normal" average earnings in the future. The attempt to forecast long-range earning power, which is itself so subject to abrupt and sudden change, should be regarded with a certain degree of skepticism. A last word of caution concerns the selection of a capitalization rate for average earnings. The capitali-

zation rate of twice the current yield on high-grade bonds constitutes a constant multiplier. What is the worth of the arbitrary selection of twice the current bond yield? Why not a higher or a
lower figure? What if a change develops in the relationship of
stock yields to bond yields? Perhaps it has proved reasonably satisfactory in the past; but this does not ensure its being an unquali-
fiedly reliable guide in the future.

Chapter 9

Conclusions

The foregoing chapters have drawn a picture—a broad survey of the theory and practice of present-day formula plans. That there has been an extensive amount of serious thinking devoted to this subject in recent years is all too apparent when one reflects on the almost infinite variety of which formula plans are capable and on the variegated methods which have been developed to make them more adaptable and responsive to the diverse needs and requirements of the investors they serve. This suggests a point of considerable significance: There is *no one* best formula plan or *one* best method. The success of a formula plan is revealed in the way it realizes the investment objectives of its sponsor. One type of plan may be ideal for one purpose; another, for a different purpose. Investors' needs and requirements are not all alike. Some investors want a conservative program, some a more liberal program. Some put primary emphasis on capital growth; others stress the importance of income. Some prefer a simple, easy-to-understand formula; others are stimulated by the challenge of complexity and more elaborate mathematical computations. Therefore, each formula plan ought to be weighed and evaluated in the light of its conformance to basic investor preferences and expectations.

It is not possible, therefore, to attempt to generalize on which

171

formula plan is best for all types of investors. However, it is possible to generalize on another and different matter pertaining to all types of plans. It is simply this: Formula plans, of whatever type, will generally produce satisfactory results if:

1. The basic presumptions enumerated in Chapter 2 are valid.
2. The investor remains loyal to his plan and refuses to be swayed by the periodical surge of his emotions.
3. The plan is kept in operation over a sufficiently long period, at least long enough to permit stock prices to traverse one or more complete cycles.

If the above points obtain, one can say with reasonable assurance that formula plans are likely to meet the conservative investor's needs and requirements more satisfactorily than are alternative solutions to the timing problem. The investor will probably feel more secure and more mentally at ease with his formula plan than he would if he had adopted some method of trend forecasting or a straightforward buy-and-hold program. But the formula investor should appreciate his plan's limitations, and he should not delude himself into expecting a fortune overnight. He should realize that he has no get-rich-quick scheme. All that should matter to him is the degree of confidence his plan affords him in the expectation of a satisfactory gain over several market cycles, if he follows his formula faithfully and steadfastly. What can be considered a satisfactory gain? The answer would no doubt vary with individual investors but, as an annual average over a long enough period, perhaps the expectation of 4 or 5 per cent capital gain plus a 3 or 4 per cent return from dividend and interest income on the stocks and bonds held in the portfolio would be considered satisfactory. That is, the total average annual yield to be expected on an account might be in the neighborhood of 8 to 9 per cent. Some years, of course, will be better than this, and others not so good, depending upon conditions in the security markets. But what we are referring to here is the *average* annual expectation.

If the formula investor can do this well, he should have no

particular reason for discouragement. To some, such an average annual gain may seem too modest and too lacking in challenge to justify bothering with formula plans in the first place. Such critics would prefer more action, to the end of making a speculative profit. But speculation involves a considerable risk, and a sizable loss is as possible an eventuality as a sizable gain. Formula plans do not, as a general rule, hold any hope of outperforming other timing methods in accomplished gains; they do strive to produce larger gains in the long run with a given amount of risk. The implicit value of a formula plan versus other methods is the reduction of risk achieved. This is the important point and the point well worth remembering when formula plans are compared to other methods. The main question is the amount of risk involved, and if a formula plan can produce a greater amount of gain with a less amount of risk, it would seem to possess a definite advantage over other timing methods.

With regard to the matter of risk, it is pertinent to compare the operation of a buy-and-hold policy and a formula plan under various conditions. If the long-term trend of stock prices were horizontal, the buy-and-hold program would produce no profit at all over one or more complete market cycles. But the formula plan, under these circumstances, would profit by selling stocks while the cyclical movement was above the long-term trend and conversely by buying stocks at progressively lower prices while the cyclical movement was below the long-term trend. And the element of risk would be less at all times with the formula plan because some portion of defensive securities would be retained throughout the cycle.

However, if the long-term trend were sharply upward without intermediate fluctuations, nothing could beat the buy-and-hold policy, for it would, at all times, be entirely aggressive. In contrast, a formula plan would not produce equivalent results because it would grow less and less aggressive as prices rose, although it would expose the investor to much less risk. If, on the other hand, the long-term trend were upward but the actual price movement developed a more or less regular cyclical pattern around the trend, the difference in achieved results between the two types of operation would be considerably narrowed.

If the long-term trend were sharply downward without intermediate fluctuations, a buy-and-hold policy would result in a serious shrinkage of capital values by the end of any given period. Since the whole fund would be invested in aggressive securities, the seriousness of the loss would be directly proportional to the amount of decline in the price movement. The formula plan, however, would fare somewhat better. Since presumably at the start only 50 per cent of the fund was aggressive, the potential shrinkage of capital value could be no greater than half that of a buy-and-hold program. Moreover, if there were some cyclical price movement around the trend, the difference in favor of the formula plan would be increased because some advantage would be taken of the fluctuations either to add to stocks gradually or to dispose of them gradually, thus realizing some degree of gain even though the long-term trend were unfavorable. If the long-term trend were declining faster than commodity prices, it would be the option of the formula investor to maintain the entire fund in cash or defensive securities until a better opportunity for buying stocks appeared. Other timing methods might not be so fortunate.

It is, then, no indictment of a formula plan to say that it did not do as well as some other method for any given period. Under certain conditions the formula does not pretend, and could not possibly hope, to do as well as one or more alternatives. But this is no reason to discard it arbitrarily. If his gain is relatively modest, at least the formula investor should have felt greater security while acquiring it, and he has, in fact, been exposed to a good deal less risk.

Moreover, in any long-term bull market, it is easy to point out the disadvantages and limitations of formula plans, particularly as the top of the movement is approached. It is easy to look back and see what one might have done by forecasting the trend or buying and holding, as against what one might have done with a formula plan. But hindsight in such a case can only be a very deceptive guide. For instance, the DJIA has been in a steady and rather sharp climb from 1949 to June–July of 1957. But did all investors have the courage and fortitude—as well as the foresight—to invest boldly when prices were at their lows in 1949? And even if they had, is it reasonable to suppose that they would have held on until today? It is a good deal more likely that they would have divested themselves of many of their holdings long before this. A formula plan, however, *requires* the investor to buy at certain times and to sell at others and it does not—or should not—require a great degree of courage or foresight, once it is established.

It should also be noted that the mere adoption of a formula plan does *not* provide an automatic solution to all of the investor's problems. It should help to improve his timing operations but it leaves the problem of selection wide open. Good security selection is a necessary concomitant to a good formula plan. The results that the plan will yield will largely be proportional to the quality of the securities that comprise the aggressive and defensive portions of the fund. The portfolio must be continuously supervised and scrutinized; desirable switches must be made when necessary; the investor must be constantly alert to opportunities to improve investment quality, to increase yield, and to eliminate deteriorating or disappointing situations by replacing them with others that offer more promise. But any prudent investor would have this problem, and he would also be faced with the perplexing problem of timing as well. For the formula investor, at least, the problem of timing is settled and he can devote all his time, if necessary, to better security selection.

Of course, formula plans do not please everybody. They are obviously not intended for the nimble speculator—the fellow who is in and out of the market all the time or the fellow who thinks he can beat the trend. They definitely do not appeal to bolder investors who are looking for large capital gains and high yields, investors to whom the profit results produced by formula plans seem to be relatively unattractive. Sometimes the instability of income, and particularly the decline in income when the greater part of the fund is shifted either to cash or to low-yielding defensive securities, makes these plans less appealing to those investors who put great store by income regularity.

To some people, too, formula plans may seem to be too complicated and to involve too much time and effort for the results achieved. To others they may seem to require too much patience, particularly when to follow them rigidly would leave the investor on the sidelines in extended periods of inactivity while actual prices were perhaps still undergoing sizable movements outside the projected range of the plans. Some formula plans, again, assume the existence of such an adequate fund to begin with that the fellow of modest means is more or less automatically eliminated. These criticisms may be perfectly valid when applied to a particular type of investor or to a particular historical time period. But they also indicate that formula plans are not designed to meet every investor's needs; they can not be considered universally adaptable to everyone's investment problems. Anyone who adopts a formula plan should be fully conscious of the method's limitations and potential pitfalls as well as the advantages he may reasonably expect from it. Certainly the author would agree that any plan calling for a certain rigidity of operation would probably not meet all future contingencies successfully in an uncertain, dynamic future. But this should not be an indictment restricted solely to formula plans. Any other timing method would also have to cope with such contingencies. But at least it seems to be a healthy development that formula plans are being looked at more critically and that their limitations are being studied and brought to light. The big difficulty seems to lie in the way in which the future trend of prices and the range of fluctuation are projected. Careful students of the problem are already conscious of the difficulties inherently involved with moving averages and visually projected trends as methods of trend-line determination. The propensity at the moment seems to be more in the direction of favoring the intrinsic-value method. More research and more experience may yet produce a method of trend determination that will perhaps prove more satisfactory than any yet developed. But just because the formula method is being subjected today to greater critical analysis should not be taken as proof that it has nothing to offer at all. It is no reason for summarily discarding the whole idea. Legitimate criticism can be constructive in pointing up not only the problems involved but also the likely paths to their solution. As more problems are solved, as more difficulties are overcome, and as more practical experience is gained, the way may gradually be cleared for more widespread public acceptance of the formula idea.

Some people are questioning formula plans today, particularly in view of the spectacular rise in the DJIA from 1953 levels to the highs of 1956–1957. Of course, the current bull market really started in 1949 but there was not much in the way of disparaging talk about variable-ratio formula plans until the upper limits of their projected ranges began to be exceeded. When the DJIA crossed 300 in early 1954 and began its steep climb, one after another of the variable-ratio plans reduced the fund to minimum stock proportions and either became immobilized (100 per cent defensive) or reverted to a constant-ratio plan, with a small percentage aggressive and a larger percentage defensive. Before this, the various plans had probably been accumulating systematic profits as the DJIA rose; after this, as the price movement continued upward, the period of questioning and of considerable misgiving developed. It began to be said that formula plans were not flexible enough, that the inability to take advantage of the continued rise was seriously limiting potential gains, that the immobilization and the prospect of a considerable period of inactivity was putting a severe strain upon the investor's patience. How many investors succumbed to the temptation to break away from their formula plans, there is no way of telling. We do know, however, that certain institutional pioneers in the field gradually departed more and more from the formula method as conditions changed, until there was hardly a vestige of the original method left. It has already been indicated that Yale University, Vassar College, and Oberlin College have given up their formula plans. On the other hand, some of the early supporters of the method are still maintaining an unshaken faith in the long run validity of their plans. The duPont Institutional Fund is still operating according to its original plan; the Keystone Seven-Step Plan is still active, and thus far the channel has not been revised; Benjamin Graham is still using his Central-value method in the operation of a portion of the fund of the Graham-Newman Corporation; Kenyon College and Syracuse University are still holding fast to their formulas; the Genstein plan is still the basis for a private-fund operation; and the First National Bank of Birmingham is apparently satisfied to continue to use its plan in connection with its various trust accounts.

No one knows for sure what the future holds in store. As long as the market continues to rise, formula plans will perhaps continue to be a target for considerable criticism. However, it is a known fact that the stock market has always fluctuated in the past. No cyclical movement has persisted forever. In the late 1920's, when people began to speak of new economic eras, the end of depressions, and permanently higher stock market levels, history now shows us that conditions were ripe for a turn. How differently did the same people speak just a few years later, in the early 1930's, when statements about permanent depression and economic stagnation in the United States were gaining widespread currency! History again shows that conditions then also were ripe for a turn. By historical analogy, we are able to discern another relationship —one revealing alternate periods in the past 15 or 20 years when formula plans were most in favor and when most out of favor. They usually were most in favor during bear markets, particularly when the price drop was steep and abrupt. A growing amount of favorable consideration was accorded formula plans in 1937, 1940, 1942, and 1946 when people, caught again in the respective price declines, were searching for a new approach to investment timing. When things righted themselves again and bull markets succeeded bear markets, formula plans came to be looked upon as too rigidly restrictive. The same sort of situation seems to be prevailing today. The author prefers to feel that the historical pattern of stock-price fluctuations will continue to manifest itself in the future as it has in the past and that, at a time yet to come, formula plans, with due allowance for their attendant limitations, may once more assume their rightful place in the repertoire of investor thinking.

Bibliography

BOOKS

1. Badger, R. E., and H. G. Guthmann, *Investment Principles and Practices*, 4th ed. Englewood Cliffs, N.J.: Prentice-Hall, Inc., 1951, chaps. 26–28.
2. Carpenter, H. G., *Investment Timing by Formula Plans*. New York: Harper & Brothers, 1943.
3. Clendenin, John C., *Introduction to Investments*, 2d ed. New York: McGraw-Hill Book Company, Inc., 1955, chap. 10.
4. Cottle, C. S., and W. T. Whitman, *Investment Timing—The Formula Plan Approach*. New York: McGraw-Hill Book Company, Inc., 1953.
5. Dewey, E. R., and E. F. Dakin, *Cycles—The Science of Prediction*. New York: Henry Holt and Company, Inc., 1947.
6. Drew, Garfield L., *New Methods for Profit in the Stock Market*. Boston: Metcalf Press, 1951.
7. Genstein, Edgar S., *Stock Market Profit Without Forecasting*. South Orange, N.J.: Investment Research Press, 1954.
8. Graham, B., and D. L. Dodd, *Security Analysis*, 3d ed. New York: McGraw-Hill Book Company, Inc., 1951.
9. ———, *The Intelligent Investor*, 2d ed. New York: Harper & Brothers, 1954.
10. Grodinsky, Julius, *Investments*. New York: The Ronald Press Company, 1953, parts 5 and 6; esp. chap. 26.
11. Hirsch, Werner Z., *Introduction to Modern Statistics*. New York: The Macmillan Company, 1957.
12. Kamm, Jacob O., *Economics of Investment*. New York: American Book Company, 1951, chaps. 21–24.
13. Merritt, Robert D., *Financial Independence through Common Stocks*. Boston: United Business Service, 1952.

14. Plum, L. V., and J. H. Humphrey, *Investment Analysis and Management*. Homewood, Ill.: Richard D. Irwin, Inc., 1951, chaps. 16–18.
15. Robbins, Sidney M., *Managing Securities*. Boston: Houghton Mifflin Company, 1954, chaps. 37, 38.
16. Sauvain, Harry C., *Investment Management*. Englewood Cliffs, N.J.: Prentice-Hall, Inc., 1953, chaps. 14–19.
17. Tomlinson, Lucile, *Practical Formulas for Successful Investing*. New York: Wilfred Funk, Inc., 1953.
18. ———, *Successful Investing Formulas*. Boston: Barron's, 1947.
19. Wilmore, Thomas F., *A Lifetime Investment Program*. New York: Harper & Brothers, 1954.
20. Wright, Wilson, *Forecasting for Profit*. New York: John Wiley & Sons, Inc., 1947.

REPORTS

21. *The duPont Institutional Investment Index*. New York: Francis I. duPont & Co., 1947.
22. *Formula Plan Investing*. Boston: Keystone Company of Boston, 1952.
23. *Monthly Investment Plan*. New York: New York Stock Exchange, 1954.

ARTICLES

24. Cottle, C. Sidney, "Factors to be Considered in Appraising Formula Plans." *Southern Economic Journal*, vol. 16, no. 1, July, 1949, pp. 62–79.
25. ——— and W. T. Whitman, "Formula Plans and the Institutional Investor." *Harvard Business Review*, vol. 28, no. 4, July, 1950, pp. 84–96.
26. ——— and ———, "Testing Formula Plans." *Journal of Finance*, vol. 6, no. 2, June, 1951, pp. 220–228.
27. Cowles, Alfred, "Can Stock Market Forecasters Forecast?" *Econometrica*, July, 1933, pp. 319–324.
28. ———, "Stock Market Forecasting." *Econometrica*, July-October, 1944, pp. 206–214.
29. Jones, A. W., "Fashions in Forecasting." *Fortune*, March, 1949, pp. 88–97.
30. Ketchum, Marshall D., "Investment Management through Formula Timing Plans." *Journal of Business*, University of Chicago, vol. 20, no. 3, July, 1947, pp. 156–169.
31. ———, "Adjustment for the Secular Trend of Stock Prices."

Journal of Business, University of Chicago, vol. 21, no. 1, January, 1948, pp. 29–49.

32. ————, "Can Life Insurance Companies Use Formula Plans?" *Journal of Business*, University of Chicago, vol. 22, no. 1, January, 1949, pp. 30–49.

33. Schneider, Henry S., "Two Formula Methods for Choosing Common Stocks." *Journal of Finance*, vol. 6, no. 2, June, 1951, pp. 229–237.

34. Solomon, Ezra, "Are Formula Plans What They Seem to Be?" *Journal of Business*, University of Chicago, vol. 21, no. 2, April, 1948, pp. 92–97.

35. Szatrowski, Zenon, "A Statistical Approach to Formula Planning." *The Analysts Journal*, May, 1955, reprint, pp. 3–7.

36. Tomlinson, Lucile, "Formulas Tested." *Barron's*, October 10, 1955, pp. 5, 6, 26.

37. Warren, Robert A., "Formula Plan Investing." *Harvard Business Review*, vol. 31, no. 1, January-February, 1953, pp. 57–69.

38. Weston, J. Fred, "Some Theoretical Aspects of Formula Timing." *Journal of Business*, University of Chicago, vol. 22, no. 4, October, 1949, pp. 249–270.

Index